MARTHA FRANCES
6405 WESTWARD APT 65
HOUSTON TX 77081

TELLING THE TRUTH

TELLING

1817

Published in San Francisco by

THE TRUTH

The Gospel as Tragedy, Comedy, and Fairy Tale

FREDERICK BUECHNER

HARPER & ROW, PUBLISHERS

New York, Hagerstown, San Francisco, London

Designed by Jim Mennick

Library of Congress Cataloging in Publication Data
Buechner, Frederick, 1926–
TELLING THE TRUTH.

   1. Preaching. 2. Communication (Theology).
I. Title.
BV4211.2.B78   251   77–10586
ISBN 0–06–061156–1

82 10 9

For May

Contents

1 ... Telling the Truth

ON January 31, 1872, Henry Ward Beecher traveled to Yale to deliver the first of the Beecher Lectures on preaching, which had been established in memory of his father. His biographer writes:

> He had a bad night, not feeling well. Went to his hotel, got his dinner, lay down to take a nap. About two o'clock he got up and began to shave without having been able to get at any plan of the lecture to be delivered within the hour. Just as he had his face lathered and was beginning to strop his razor, the whole thing came out of the clouds and dawned on him. He dropped his razor, seized his pencil, and dashed off the memoranda for it and afterwards cut himself badly, he said, thinking it out.[1]

And well the old pulpiteer might have cut himself with his razor because part of the inner world that his lecture came from, among the clouds that it suddenly dawned on him out of, was the deep trouble that he was in or the deep trouble that was in him. The gossip about his relationship with the wife of one of his parishioners had left the whispering stage and was beginning to appear more or less directly in print. Compromising letters were being handed around and tearful confessions made. People were taking sides. Charges were being formulated. A public trial for adultery was not far off. It was not just his reputation and career that were in danger but in some measure the church itself—everything he believed in and stood for and had come to Yale to talk about.

So when he stood there looking into the hotel mirror with soap on his face and a razor in his hand, part of what he saw was his own shame and horror, the sight of his own folly, the judgment one can imagine he found even harder to bear than God's, which was his own judgment on himself, because whereas God is merciful, we are none of us very good at showing mercy on ourselves. Henry Ward Beecher cut himself with his razor and wrote out notes for that first Beecher Lecture in blood because, whatever else he was or aspired to be or was famous for being, he was a man of flesh and blood, and so were all the men who over the years traveled to New Haven after him to deliver the same lectures.

Phillips Brooks, Dean Inge, Harry Emerson Fosdick, Reinhold Niebuhr—the whole distinguished procession. One thinks of them all kissing their wives good-bye, if they had wives to kiss, packing their bags, and setting off to deliver their lectures on preaching, on what it means to preach, on how to preach, on what to preach, on maybe even why to

preach at all when sometimes almost anything else seems to
be more relevant and make more sense. One thinks of how
each of them left his world behind to go to Connecticut and
yet at the same time did not leave his world behind because
of course no one ever can. You can kiss your family and
friends good-bye and put miles between you, but at the
same time you carry them with you in your heart, your
mind, your stomach, because you do not just live in a world
but a world lives in you. You are a world. All of those men
were worlds in their time with their whiskers on their chins,
some of them, their clean shirts, their steel-rimmed glasses,
their freshly polished shoes. As surely as each of them
brought a toothbrush with him, he also brought with him
his loves and hates, his fears of death and his fears of life,
his anxieties, his longings, his pride, his dark doubts. Each
carried his world on his back the way a snail carries his
shell, and so did the ones who traveled to New Haven to
hear them lecture.

So one thinks of them, too, the hearers as well as the
givers of lectures. There were fat ones and thin ones, old
ones and young ones, happy ones and sad ones, some bright
and some not so bright. They also brought their worlds with
them and when they looked in their mirrors saw, if not
adulteries of the flesh, then adulteries of the spirit, failures
of faith, hope, love, failures of courage. Like Henry Ward
Beecher, like all of us, each of them too had bled a little.
"All have sinned" (Rom. 3:23), Saint Paul says, which is
another way of saying it, or all are human, which is another.
We have all cut ourselves. We all labor and are heavy laden
under the burden of being human or at least of being on the
way, we hope, to being human.

The distances between the inner world that each of us
is are greater in their way than the distances between the

outer worlds of interstellar space, but in another way, the worlds of all of us are also the same world. An occasional bad night, not feeling well. A ten o'clock arrival, a two o'clock nap. The same old face in the mirror day after day. An empty feeling in the pit of the stomach. A little blood. We are all of us in it together, and it is in us all. So if preachers or lecturers are to say anything that really matters to anyone including themselves, they must say it not just to the public part of us that considers interesting thoughts about the Gospel and how to preach it, but to the private, inner part too, to the part of us all where our dreams come from, both our good dreams and our bad dreams, the inner part where thoughts mean less than images, elucidation less than evocation, where our concern is less with how the Gospel is to be preached than with what the Gospel is and what it is to us. They must address themselves to the fullness of who we are and to the emptiness too, the emptiness where grace and peace belong but mostly are not, because terrible as well as wonderful things have happened to us all.

In Shakespeare's *King Lear*, which is one of the mightiest of all preachments, terrible as well as wonderful things happen too. It is the "poor naked wretches" of the world, as Lear calls them, who somehow survive in spirit and the rich and powerful who are finally brought down by their own power. It is the madmen and fools who turn out to be wise and the wise and worldly who turn out to be fools. Foolish old Gloucester has his eyes put out but then suddenly, for the first time, sees the truth about himself and his sons. Mad old Lear loses his crown and his kingdom but at the last becomes for the first time truly a king. The villainy of the bad sisters is unmasked at last, and the purity of the good sister shines out in all its splendor. But then catastrophe occurs, and, in the last act, the good and the bad, the wise and the foolish, the weak and the strong, all die alike, and the stage is so littered with corpses that there is nobody much left except Edgar to stammer the curtain down as best he can. What he says is this:

> The weight of this sad time we must obey
> Speak what we feel, not what we ought to say.
> 　　　　[5.3.324–325]

They are not the most powerful lines in the play, but they are among the most telling because in them it would seem that Shakespeare is telling us something about himself and about the way he wrote his play. What he has done in *Lear* is to look as deep as he can into the dark and ambiguous heart of things and then to body forth an impassioned statement about what he has found there which on its own scale approaches being as rich and complex and uncompromising as what he has found, a statement in which he is less concerned with matters of form and clarity and good taste than he is simply with telling the truth. He risks making a terrible fool of himself in *Lear,* and in scenes like the one where blind Gloucester thinks he is throwing himself off a cliff when there actually is no cliff, or where Lear starts tearing his clothes off and babbling nonsense, a single titter from the audience could destroy everything. But in the interests of truth-telling, there seems to be no risk that Shakespeare is not willing to run as if from the conviction that if the truth is worth telling, it is worth making a fool of yourself to tell. He could have made his play simpler. He could have made it a drama primarily of despair because in the meaningless, grotesque deaths of good and bad alike there is despair enough for anybody. Or he could have made it a drama primarily of hope because whereas the bad are transformed by their suffering into beasts at each other's throats, the good, however briefly and precariously, are hallowed by it. Like Edgar, Shakespeare may well have thought that for the sake of unity, clarity, dramatic effect, for the sake of his own sanity even, let alone his reputation, what he *ought* to have said in his play was one or the other of these—despair or hope—but instead what he said was both of them and thus something in a way more than, and different from, either. What he said was what in the deepest sense he truly felt. He looked into the dark heart of things, which is to say into his own heart and into our hearts, too, and told as close to the whole truth as he was able.

Insofar as the truth is tragic, he told a tragedy of men and women suffering more than even their own folly and wickedness seem to merit. Insofar as the truth is comic, both in the sense of a kind of terrible funniness and of a happy end to all that is terrible, he told a comedy of madmen and fools. Insofar as the truth transcends all such distinctions and points beyond itself, he told a kind of fairy tale where everybody is disguised as something he or she is not and only at the end are all disguises stripped away so that finally all are revealed for what they truly are, and like the beast in "Beauty and the Beast," the old king, with Cordelia in her beauty dead in his arms, is finally turned into a human being.

Not only preachers like old Beecher but anyone who tries to express the Gospel in words, even if only to himself, has much to learn here. The weight of these sad times we must obey and must obey just because they are sad times, sad and bewildering times for people who try to hold on to the Gospel and witness to it somehow when in so many ways the weight of our sadness all but crushes the life out of it. One wonders if there is anything more crucial for the preacher to do than to obey the sadness of our times by taking it into account without equivocation or subterfuge, by speaking out of our times and into our times not just what we ought to say about the Gospel, not just what it would appear to be in the interests of the Gospel for us to say, but what we have ourselves felt about it, experienced of it. It is possible to think of the Gospel and our preaching of it as, above all and at no matter what risk, a speaking of the truth about the way things are. And it is possible to think of that truth as tragedy, as comedy, and as fairy tale.

The Gospel is bad news before it is good news. It is the news that man is a sinner, to use the old word, that he is evil in the imagination of his heart, that when he looks in the mirror all in a lather what he sees is at least eight parts chicken, phony, slob. That is the tragedy. But it is also the news that he is loved anyway, cherished, forgiven, bleeding to be sure, but also bled for. That is the comedy. And yet, so what? So what if even in his sin the slob is loved and forgiven when the very mark and substance of his sin and of his slobbery is that he keeps turning down the love and forgiveness because he either doesn't believe them or doesn't want them or just doesn't give a damn? In answer, the news of the Gospel is that extraordinary things happen to him just as in fairy tales extraordinary things happen. Henry Ward Beecher cheats on his wife, his God, himself, but manages to keep on bringing the Gospel to life for people anyway, maybe even for himself. Lear goes berserk on a heath but comes out of it for a few brief hours every inch a king. Zaccheus climbs up a sycamore tree a crook and climbs down a saint. Paul sets out a hatchet man for the Pharisees and comes back a fool for Christ. It is impossible for anybody to leave behind the darkness of the world he carries on his back like a snail, but for God all things are possible. That is the fairy tale. All together they are the truth.

But to preach the Gospel is not just to tell the truth but to tell the truth in love, and to tell the truth in love means to tell it with concern not only for the truth that is being told but with concern also for the people it is being told to. So it is crucial to keep them in mind too, the hearers of the tragic, the comic, the fairy-tale truth. Who are they? What is going on inside them? What is happening behind their faces where they have cut themselves to make them strain to hear the truth if it is told? The preacher must always try to feel what it is like to live inside the skins of the people he is preaching to, to hear the truth as they hear it. That is not as hard as it sounds because, of course, he is himself a hearer of truth as well as a teller of truth, and he listens out of the same emptiness as they do for a truth to fill him and make him true. So at the deepest level all hearers of the truth are the same hearer, and when I try to picture him or her, what I picture is the one who is famous for having asked to hear, who took a long drag on his cigarette and through narrowed eyes asked, "What is truth?" (John 18:38). One might do worse than to start with him.

He is Pontius Pilate, of course. He is the procurator of Judea. On the day that he asks his famous question, there are other things too that he has seen and done. He makes his first major decision before he has even had his breakfast. While still in his pajamas, he walks downstairs to the bar closet where he keeps extra cigarettes, takes the two and a half cartons that he finds there and puts them out with the trash. There is the remains of a pack in the pocket of his dinner jacket and some loose ones lying around the house in various cigarette boxes. All of these he carefully destroys, slitting them open with his thumbnail and flushing the tobacco down the toilet. After dinner the evening before, the talk turned to politics, and he was up for hours, talking and smoking, so that when he awoke, his tongue felt hot and dry, his whole chest raw inside like a wound. He knows about the surgeon general's warning. He has seen the usual photographs of a smoker's lungs. He has been a three-pack-a-day man for better or worse than thirty years so his prebreakfast decision is a decision for life against death, and he sees it as his death that he slits open with his thumbnail and flushes away.

It is a good start, and he feels better for it. Not even the morning paper upsets him, leafing through it in the back seat of the limousine as he is driven into the city. It contains the usual grim recital—poverty, crime, disease, corruption in high places, ignorance and superstition and indifference in low places and everywhere else—but he feels for the moment wonderfully insulated from it as the car rolls along and he glances out at the world from time to time through the tinted windows. Children are playing in the street, heavily armed policemen patrolling the seedier neighborhoods, sightseers feeding pigeons outside the temple gates. He is essentially a law-and-order man, and he is maintaining them as best he can. If the malcontents, the eggheads, and bleeding hearts, want to carry on about rottenness at the heart of things, that is their business. His concern is with rottenness in the streets, and his business is to keep the ship afloat from day to day. All in all he is not doing a bad job of it. There are no major complaints from Rome. The Jews are happy enough with their Jewish puppets. And he himself, if not exactly happy, is happy enough.

When he was a young man, he dreamed of greater things than a provincial procuratorship, but he could have done a lot worse. He is a friend of Caesar's. His sons have had the best education money could buy. His wife is subject to troubling dreams, but she is in the hands of a good analyst. Their marriage is not what it once was, but she lets him go his own way, and he has found other ways to go. He comforts her by saying that the day is not far off when they can retire to the villa outside Ostia to enjoy visits from the children and grandchildren, the evening martini, the walk along the beach. In the meantime he has appointments to keep, and he keeps them.

The chief of the occupational forces is in a sweat because the high holidays are upon them and he expects trouble from the fanatics. The Jewish God, not knowing which side his matzoh is buttered on, wants Rome out, wants the peace that passeth all understanding for his people instead of the Pax Romana. Pilate starts to reach for a cigarette and then remembers. He picks up a pencil instead. He says that what passeth his understanding is the Jews themselves, who have never had it so good. He says that what passeth his understanding is how they can go on knocking themselves out for a God who runs history when it is precisely history that has run them over and left them with their ancient superstitions as much an anachronism as an Egyptian mummy or a stone ax. Besides, he says, Caesar is God. The chief of the occupational forces is a straight party-line man with an eye for promotion, and Pilate does not quite permit himself a wink as he says it. Caesar is God, he says, with only the faintest flicker of a smile. It is not returned, and he orders the guard doubled around the temple and the whole garrison put on the alert until Passover passes over.

The tax people come in full of the usual excuses. You can't get blood out of a stone, they say, and you can't make a Roman silk purse out of the ear of a Jewish sow. A man comes in with a scheme for an aqueduct to solve the city's water problem. It will pass through land which he is prepared to sell at considerable personal sacrifice. There is some kind of epidemic in the old slave district, and there are complaints about bodies left in the streets to draw flies and packs of orphaned children scavenging among them for food. There has been some kind of demonstration at one of the city gates with some up-country messiah at the center of it, and the question is how to handle it without making it worse. The Jews are playing it safe by passing the buck to Caesar, and "There is no God, and Caesar is his name," Pilate permits himself to say this time but only to his secretary because she is young and pretty and stupid and won't get it anyway. He says he will see the man himself if that's what they want. If they want him to see their God, he will see him too. The more the merrier.

The secretary lowers her eyes under his steady, bland gaze like a girl in a convent, but he has reason to know that if there was ever a convent, she has come a long way since and wouldn't need more than a nod from him to come a good bit farther still. He is tempted for a moment to give her that nod but is deterred by his knowledge that a man needs as much singleness of purpose to be unfaithful to his wife as he needs to be faithful to her, and for the moment the only purpose he can bring himself to take seriously is lunch, which he eats quickly and alone at his desk. Roman beer, cold chicken with mayonnaise, two hard-boiled eggs, and if smoking doesn't get him, he thinks, cholesterol will. He is already older than his father lived to be, and bad hearts run in the family. When he is through eating, he would trade the Ostian villa for a cigarette, but cigarettes are death, and he has flushed them all away for the sake of life. It is a sacrifice, he hopes, that will prove worth the making.

A phone call comes through from his wife. She tells him that one of the horses has gotten foundered and has to be put down. She doesn't give a hoot about horses, but as she runs on and on about it, all of a sudden her voice goes queer and thick, and he realizes that she is weeping. He can see her sitting there with the receiver cradled between her ear and her shoulder so that she can light a cigarette as she always does when she starts to cry. He can almost smell the smoke as she lights it and then starts talking again. He closes his eyes and tries to think of something to distract her with, but nothing comes.

She is apologizing for bothering him, for weeping, apologizing for her life. She has had a bad night, the same dark dreams. . . . As she talks, he swivels around in his chair to look out the window behind him. Down in the courtyard a ragged child is talking to one of the soldiers, and he wonders if it can be one of the epidemic children, the disease clinging to its clothes like lice. A pigeon perched on the windowsill fans one wing out, then tucks it in again. When his wife finally hangs up and he swings back to his desk, he finds he is no longer alone. They have brought the up-country messiah in for questioning. Pilate is caught off-guard, and before he knows what he is doing, he takes a cigarette from an onyx box on his desk and lights it.

The man stands in front of the desk with his hands tied behind his back. You can see that he has been roughed up a little. His upper lip is absurdly puffed out and one eye is swollen shut. He looks unwashed and smells unwashed. His feet are bare—big,flat peasant feet although the man himself is not big. There is something almost comic about the way he stands there, bent slightly forward because of the way his hands are tied and goggling down at the floor through his one good eye as if he is looking for something he has lost, a button off his shirt or a dime somebody slipped him for a cup of coffee. If there were just the two of them, Pilate thinks, he would give him his carfare and send him back to the sticks where he came from, but the guards are watching, and on the wall the official portrait of Tiberius Caesar is watching, the fat, powdered face, the toothy imperial smile, so he goes through the formalities.

"So you're the king of the Jews," he says. "The head Jew," because there hasn't been one of them yet who hasn't made that his claim—David come back to give Judea back to the Jews.

The man says, "It's not this world I'm king of," but his accent is so thick that Pilate hardly gets it, the accent together with what they have done to his upper lip. As if he has a mouth full of stones, he says, "I've come to bear witness to the truth," and at that the procurator of Judea takes such a deep drag on his filter tip that his head swims and for a moment he's afraid he may faint.

He pushes back from the desk and crosses his legs. There is the papery rustle of wings as the pigeon flutters off the sill and floats down toward the cobbles. Standing by the door, the guards aren't paying much attention. One of them is picking his nose, the other staring up at the ceiling. Cigarette smoke drifts over the surface of the desk—the picture of his wife when she still had her looks, the onyx box from Caesar, the clay plaque with the imprint of his first son's hand on it, made while he was still a child in nursery school. Pilate squints at the man through the smoke and asks his question.

He asks it half because he would give as much as even

his life to hear the answer and half because he believes
there is no answer and would give a good deal to hear that
too because it would mean just one thing less to have to
worry about. He says, "What is truth?" and by way of an
answer, the man with the split lip doesn't say a blessed
thing. Or else his not saying anything, that is the blessed
thing. You could hear a pin drop in the big, high-ceilinged
room with Tiberius grinning down from the wall like a
pumpkin, that one cigarette a little unsteady between the
procurator's yellowed fingertips.

The one who hears the truth that is silence before it is a
word is Pilate, and he hears it because he has asked to hear
it, and he has asked to hear it—"What is truth?" he asks—
because in a world of many truths and half truths, he is
hungry for truth itself or, failing that, at least for the truth
that there is no truth. We are all of us Pilate in our asking
after truth, and when we come to church to ask it, the
preacher would do well to answer us also with silence
because the truth and the Gospel are one, and before the
Gospel is a word, it too like truth is silence—not an
ordinary silence, silence as nothing to hear, but silence that
makes itself heard if you listen to it the way Pilate listens to
the silence of the man with the split lip. The Gospel that is
truth is good news, but before it is good news, let us say
that it is just news. Let us say that it is the evening news,
the television news, but with the sound turned off.

Picture that then, the video without the audio, the news
with, for the moment, no words to explain it or explain it
away, no words to cushion or sharpen the shock of it, no
definition given to dispose of it with such as a fire, a battle,
a strike, a treaty, a beauty, an accident. Just the thing itself,
life itself, or as much of it as the screen can hold, flickering
away in the dark of the room. A man is making a speech

outside on a flight of stone steps with one fist going up and down, his lips moving, a single wisp of hair lifted up by the breeze like a feather, and there is a crowd watching him or not watching him as the spirit moves them or fails to move them. They are black and white, men and women, and even some of the ones who are watching him seem to have their eyes turned inward as though they are watching something else inside, listening to some other voice. Somewhere else jerry-built houses lie in ruin, and a fat woman in a Mother Hubbard stands in what was once a doorway with a cat in her arms, behind her a man in a T-shirt with a caved-in mouth. A beautiful young woman in a long dress sits down at a piano, and a pair of blacks carrying a body on a stretcher between them hotfoot it down a city street in a running crouch while from high windows snipers' bullets fly out silent as a dream. A great ship cuts through the water with many flags. A whole mountainside is awash with flame. A girl in a picture hat raises a pair of binoculars to her eyes.

Or make the TV screen a home-movie screen instead, and there he is, the old gentleman himself, with no idea in the world that it is the last summer he will ever be around to be around in. He is sitting on the lawn in a canvas deck chair with an old Panama on his head and a cigar in his hand as a woman in a bathing suit fills the screen to hand him a piece of birthday cake. It is snowing, and down the path comes a figure that it takes you a moment or two to recognize as yourself. You are pulling a sled behind you, and on the sled with his tasseled cap on cockeyed like a drunk is a small child you would have given maybe even your life for if it had somehow come to that and might even give your life for still although he is no longer a small child now but some kind of crazy dropout, bearded, drifting around from job to job in search, he says, of himself, in search perhaps really of you if the truth were known, that particular truth.

A particular truth can be stated in words—that life is better than death and love than hate, that there is a god or is not, that light travels faster than sound and cancer can sometimes be cured if you discover it in time. But truth itself is another matter, the truth that Pilate asked for, tired and bored and depressed by his long day. Truth itself cannot be stated. Truth simply is, and is what is, the good with the bad, the joy with the despair, the presence and absence of God, the swollen eye, the bird pecking the cobbles for crumbs. Before it is a word, the Gospel that is truth is silence, a pregnant silence in its ninth month, and in answer to Pilate's question, Jesus keeps silent, even with his hands tied behind him manages somehow to hold silence out like a terrible gift.

When he comes riding into the city on a mule, the cry goes up, "Blessed be the king that cometh in the name of the Lord" (Luke 19:38), and the Pharisees say, "Master, rebuke thy disciples" (Luke 29:38), and Jesus says, "I tell you, if these were silent, the very stones would cry out" (Luke 19:40). The point is, of course, that the stones do cry out. The mountain, the flames, cry out, the pretty girl at the piano cries out, and the child being born into his first summer, the old man smoking his last summer down to the butt like a cigar without knowing that it is his last summer. They all cry out truth, and their cry is wordless and silent and devastating. As somebody said, God does not sign his sunsets the way Turner did, nor does he arrange the stars to spell out messages of comfort. What is truth? Life is truth, the life of the world, your own life, and the life inside the world you are. The task of the preacher is to hold up life to us; by whatever gifts he or she has of imagination, eloquence, simple candor, to create images of life through which we can somehow see into the wordless truth of our lives. Before the Gospel is good news, it is simply the news that that's the way it is, whatever day it is of whatever year.

The crazy Zen monk holds a stick in his hand and says, "What have I got in my hand?" and the eager searcher after truth but only after a particular truth says, "It is a stick." Then the monk hits the man over the head with the stick as he richly deserves and says, "No, *that's* what it is," or doesn't even bother to say it. Pilate asks Jesus what is truth —is it what Plato said, or Maimonides, or Aquinas, or Tillich, or Henry Ward Beecher?—and what Jesus hits Pilate over the head with is Pilate himself. Jesus just stands there in silence in a way that throws Pilate back on his own silence, the truth of himself. What Jesus lets his silence say is that truth is what words can't tell but only tell about, what images can only point to. The weight of these sad times is the weight of their eloquent silence, and even when you turn the sound back on again and Eric Sevareid or Shakespeare or Billy Graham starts putting words to things, behind the words the silence of the stones cries out like thunder.

One thinks of the prophets of Israel, of Isaiah, Jeremiah, Amos, all of them. They were par excellence the putters of words to things, and the words they put are so thunderous with rage and exultation, with terrible denunciations and terrible promises, that if you are not careful, they drown out everything else there is in the Old Testament and in the prophets themselves. At the level of their words, it is not truth they are telling but particular truths. They are telling about the nations and naming names, telling about Assyria,

Babylon, Egypt, Persia, and, above all, about Israel as a
nation, and the truth they are telling until the veins stand
out on their necks and their voices grow hoarse is the truth
that by playing power politics Israel is not only bringing
about her own destruction as a nation but is acting against
her holy destiny, which is to be not a nation among nations
but a nation of priests, whose calling it is to be a light to
the world. At the level of words, the prophets speak
historical, political, theological, and, of course, ethical truths
as powerfully as anyone has ever spoken them and as
daringly, daring even to put their truths into the mouth of
God himself. "I hate, I despise your feasts, and I take no
delight in your solemn assemblies," Amos has God say, "but
let justice roll down like mighty waters and righteousness
like an ever-flowing stream" (Amos. 5:21–24). Nobody
before or since has ever used words to express more
powerfully than they our injustice and unrighteousness, our
hardness of heart, our pride, our complacency, our
hypocrisy, our idolatry, our shallowness, our faithlessness.
These particular truths that the prophets speak were crucial
for their own times and are crucial also for ours, and any
preacher who does not speak them in his own right, naming
names including his own name, any religious person who
does not heave them at the injustice and unrighteousness of
his own time and of himself, runs the risk of being
irrelevant, sentimental, a bag of wind. But, at the same time,
they are only truths. They are not the truth that Pilate
asked for just in case there happened to be any. They are
not truth itself, Gospel truth. They are not news because
even in the prophets' day they were not new.

But in addition to particular truths, the prophets spoke
truth, too, and that was when they were most truly
prophetic. They did not speak the good news because the

good news had not broken yet, but they spoke news. They put words to things until their teeth rattled, but beneath the words they put, or deep within their words, something rings out which is new because it is timeless, the silence rings out, the truth that is unutterable, that is mystery, that is the way things are, and the reason it rings out seems to be that the language the prophets use is essentially the language of poetry, which more than polemics or philosophy, logic or theology, is the language of truth.

You have only to hear it to recognize it because even in the stately cadences of seventeenth-century English it is there, let alone in the volcanic gutturals of ancient Hebrew. "Hast thou not known?" says Isaiah. "Hast thou not heard, that the everlasting God, the Lord, the creator of the ends of the earth, fainteth not, neither is weary? There is no searching of his understanding. He giveth power to the faint, and to them that have no might he increaseth strength. Even the youths shall faint and be weary, and the young men shall utterly fail; but they that wait upon the Lord shall renew their strength. They shall mount up on wings like eagles. They shall run and not be weary. They shall walk and not faint" (Isa. 40: 28–31).

Hosea speaks with the dying fall of his own very different images. "I taught Ephraim also to walk, taking them by their arms, but they knew not that I healed them. I drew them with the cords of compassion, with bands of love, and I became as one who eases the yoke on their jaws, and I bent down to them and fed them. They shall return to the land of Egypt, and Assyria shall be their king, because they have refused to turn to me. The sword shall rage against their cities, consume the bars of their gates, and devour their fortresses. Yet how shall I give thee up, O Ephraim? How can I hand you over, O Israel? Mine heart is

turned within me. My repentings are kindled within me. I
will not execute the fierceness of my anger, and I will not
return to destroy Israel, because I am God and not man, the
holy one in the midst of thee . . . (Hos. 11:3–9).

At the highest reach of his wildest hope, Isaiah speaks
also in poetry. "There shall be no more thence an infant that
lives but a few days nor an old man that hath not filled out
his days. They shall not build and another inhabit. They
shall not plant and another eat. They shall not labor in vain
nor being forth trouble, and it shall come to pass that before
they call, I will answer. While they are yet speaking, I will
hear. The wolf and the lamb shall feed together, and the
lion shall eat straw like the bullock, and dust shall be the
serpent's food. They shall not hurt nor destroy in all my
holy mountain, saith the Lord" (Isa. 65:20–25 passim.).

At the lowest ebb of his despair, it is a poem that
Jeremiah writes. "O Lord, thou hast deceived me, and I was
deceived. Thou art stronger than I and hast prevailed. I am
in derision daily. Everyone mocketh me. . . . I will not make
mention of thee nor speak any more in thy name. But thy
word was in my heart as a burning fire shut up in my
bones, and I was weary with forebearing, and I could not
stay. . . . Cursed be the day wherein I was born. Let not the
day where in my mother bare me be blessed. . . . Wherefore
came I forth out of the womb to see labor and sorrow, that
my days should be consumed with shame?" (Jer. 20:7–18).

And finally the greatest poem of them all. "Who has
believed our report and to whom is the arm of the Lord
revealed? For he shall grow up before him as a tender plant
and as a root out of a dry ground. He hath no form or
comeliness, and when we shall see him, there is no beauty
that we shall desire him. He is despised and rejected of men,
a man of sorrows and acquainted with grief, and we hid as

it were our faces from him. He was despised and we esteemed him not. . . . But he was wounded for our transgressions. He was bruised for our iniquities. Upon him was the chastisement that made us whole, and with his stripes we are healed" (Isa. 53:2–5).

At the level of words, what do they say, these prophet-preachers? They say this and they say that. They say things that are relevant, lacerating, profound, beautiful, spine-chilling, and more besides. They put words to both the wonder and the horror of the world, and the words can be looked up in the dictionary or the biblical commentary and can be interpreted, passed on, understood, but because these words are poetry, are image and symbol as well as meaning, are sound and rhythm, maybe above all are passion, they set echoes going the way a choir in a great cathderal does, only it is we who become the cathedral and in us that the words echo.

Ethically, politically, religiously, the prophets say what they ought to say, to use Shakespeare's phrase again, but beyond and even more crucial than that they say what they feel in a language that even across all the centuries and through all the translations and mistranslations causes us to feel them, too. At their most truly prophetic they speak things that my guess is that even they themselves did not entirely understand because they are things that are of truth itself rather than of particular truths, truth itself which cannot finally be understood but only experienced. It is the experience that they stun us with, speaking it out in poetry which transcends all other language in its power to open the doors of the heart. The man of sorrows and acquainted with grief. The one with the cauliflower ear and the split lip. By whose swollen eye and ruptured spleen we are somehow healed. Who can put a word to him and who needs to?

They simply hold him up to our gaze. At their most poetic
and powerful they do not say something as much as they
make something happen.

So the sermon hymn comes to a close with a somewhat
unsteady amen, and the organist gestures the choir to sit
down. Fresh from breakfast with his wife and children and a
quick runthrough of the Sunday papers, the preacher climbs
the steps to the pulpit with his sermon in his hand. He
hikes his black robe up at the knee so he will not trip over
it on the way up. His mouth is a little dry. He has cut
himself shaving. He feels as if he has swallowed an anchor.
If it weren't for the honor of the thing, he would just as
soon be somewhere else.

In the front pews the old ladies turn up their hearing
aids, and a young lady slips her six year old a Lifesaver and
a Magic Marker. A college sophomore home for vacation,
who is there because he was dragged there, slumps forward
with his chin in his hand. The vice-president of a bank who
twice that week has seriously contemplated suicide places
his hymnal in the rack. A pregnant girl feels the life stir
inside her. A high-school math teacher, who for twenty
years has managed to keep his homosexuality a secret for
the most part even from himself, creases his order of service
down the center with his thumbnail and tucks it under his
knee. Pilate is there. The aqueduct man is there who has
indicated that he will make it worth his while if his people
get the contract, and Henry Ward Beecher is there. It is a
busman's holiday for him. The vestry has urged him to take
a week off for a badly needed rest, and he has come to hear
how somebody else does it for a change. It is not that he
doesn't love his wife, but just that, pushing sixty, he has
been caught preposterously off-guard by someone who lets
him open his heart to her, someone willing in her beauty to

hear out the old spellbinder, who as a minister has never had anybody much to minister to him. King Lear is there with a bit of dried egg on his tie and weak kidneys.

The preacher pulls the little cord that turns on the lectern light and deals out his note cards like a riverboat gambler. The stakes have never been higher. Two minutes from now he may have lost his listeners completely to their own thoughts, but at this minute he has them in the palm of his hand. The silence in the shabby church is deafening because everybody is listening to it. Everybody is listening including even himself. Everybody knows the kind of things he has told them before and not told them, but who knows what this time, out of the silence, he will tell them?

Let him tell them the truth. Before the Gospel is a word, it is silence. It is the silence of their own lives and of his life. It is life with the sound turned off so that for a moment or two you can experience it not in terms of the words you make it bearable by but for the unutterable mystery that it is. Let him say, "Be silent and know that I am God, saith the Lord" (Ps. 46:10). Be silent and know that even by my silence and absence I am known. Be silent and listen to the stones cry out.

Out of the silence let the only real news come, which is sad news before it is glad news and that is fairy tale last of all. The preacher is not brave enough to be literally silent for long, and since it is his calling to speak the truth with love, even if he were brave enough, he would not be silent for long because we are none of us very good at silence. It says too much. So let him use words, but, in addition to using them to explain, expound, exhort, let him use them to evoke, to set us dreaming as well as thinking, to use words as at their most prophetic and truthful, the prophets used them to stir in us memories and longings and intuitions that we starve for without knowing that we starve. Let him use words which do not only try to give answers to the questions that we ask or ought to ask but which help us to hear the questions that we do not have words for asking and to hear the silence that those questions rise out of and the silence that is the answer to those questions. Drawing on nothing fancier than the poetry of his own life, let him use words and images that help make the surface of our lives transparent to the truth that lies deep within them, which is the wordless truth of who we are and who God is and the Gospel of our meeting.

II . . . The Gospel
as Tragedy

THE preaching of the Gospel is a telling of the truth or
the putting of a sort of frame of words around the silence
that is truth because truth in the sense of fullness, of the
way things are, can at best be only pointed to by the
language of poetry—of metaphor, image, symbol—as it is
used in the prophets of the Old Testament and elsewhere.
Before the Gospel is a word, it is a silence, a kind of
presenting of life itself so that we see it not for what at
various times we call it—meaningless or meaningful, absurd,
beautiful—but for what it truly is in all its complexity,
simplicity, mystery. The silence of Jesus in answer to Pilate's
question about truth seems such a presenting as does also in
a way the silence of the television news with the sound
turned off—the real news is what we see and feel, not what
Walter Cronkite tells us—or the silence the Psalmist means

when he says, "Be silent and know that I am God." In each case it is a silence that demands to be heard because it is a presented silence, and the preacher must somehow himself present this silence and mystery of truth by speaking what he feels, not what he ought to say, by speaking forth not only the light and the hope of it but the darkness as well, all of it, because the Gospel has to do with all of it. Since words are his chief instrument, words are what he chiefly has to use but remembering always that the silence that his words frame—the silence that his words are born out of and that his words break and that his words are swallowed up by—may well convey the mystery of truth better than the words themselves can just as the empty space inside a church may well convey better than all the art and architecture of a church the mystery of that in which we live and move and have our being. We put frames of words around silence and shells of stone and wood around emptiness, but it is the silence, the emptiness themselves, that finally matter and out of which the Gospel comes as word.

It comes as a tragic word, among other things, and again it is in *King Lear* that we find an epigraph, another set of lines, but instead of quoting them directly, I want to come at them as they are quoted in the course of a scene from a novel. The scene takes place in a high-school English class where a group of seniors are being taught the play by a teacher who is himself the narrator of the scene. He describes it this way:

> The *Lear* class had gone better than usual. It was the third act that was up for grabs that day—Lear on the heath with Kent and the Fool, the storm coming up— and nothing could have seemed more remote from our

condition, yet there was a moment or two when for
some reason it worked, came alive, no thanks to me.
There they all sat drowsy and full of lunch. There was
a gym class going on outside. You could hear somebody
calling out calisthenics, *one* and two, and *one* and two.
There was a bumblebee softly bumping his way back
and forth across the ceiling, but nobody was paying
much attention to him. I sat on the windowsill in my
shirt sleeves asking some boring questions somebody
had written in the margin of my teaching copy and
wondering idly who had written them and when, and
not caring much whether anyone tried to answer them
or not. "What evidence do you find in Act Three for a
significant change in Lear's character?" was one of the
questions, and a fat boy named William Urquhart
surprised me by answering it. He was sitting all bent
over with his head in his arms on the desk, and I'd
thought he was asleep. His voice came out muffled by
his arm. He said, "He's gotten kinder."

I said, "What makes you think so?"

The second question coming so quick on the heels
of the one he'd just answered was more than William
Urquhart had bargained for, and he shifted his head to
the other arm without saying anything. You could see
where his cheek had gotten all moist and red where
he'd been lying on it, and there was the imprint of
wrinkles from his sleeve.

The ball was picked up by a boy named Greg
Dixon. He was the pimpliest member of the class and
the least popular. He said, "Well, when it starts to rain,
he thinks about the Fool keeping dry, too. He says it
right here someplace. 'Come on, my boy. How dost, my
boy?' Here it is. He says, 'Poor fool and knave, I have

one part in my heart / That's sorry yet for thee' He's getting kinder to people, just like Urquhart said."

"Also, he says a prayer for people." It was Laura Fleischman who had spoken up this time. She always sat in the back row next to a good-looking basketball player named Carl West, who knew he could have any girl in the class but for the time being anyway had settled for her. Usually she didn't speak at all or spoke with a kind of startled breathiness as if she was surprised herself that anything beside Carl West could get a rise out of her.

Somebody horselaughed not so much at what she'd said, I thought, as at the fact that it was she who'd said it. Carl West sat there beside her with his stocking feet stretched out as far as they would go and his head lolling back as if to watch the bee on the ceiling.

"Nobody says a prayer in my book," Greg Dixon said.

"Line 35," Laura Fleischman said.

"That's no prayer," Greg Dixon said. "That's not like any prayer I ever heard of. It doesn't even say God in it."

I said, "Go ahead and read it out aloud will you, Laura,"

Carl West sat humped over sideways now as far from Laura Fleischman as he could get without standing up and changing his seat. He was staring down at the wooden writing arm, tracing some scar on it over and over again with one finger.

In a small, half-apologetic voice with the calisthenic count going on in the background, she read;

Poor naked wretches, wheresoe'er you are,
That bide the pelting of this pitiless storm,

> How shall your houseless heads and unfed sides,
> Your loop'd and window'd raggedness, defend you
> From seasons such as these?

Every person has one particular time in his life when he is more beautiful than he is ever going to be again. For some it is at seven, for others at seventeen or seventy, and as Laura Fleischman read out loud from Shakespeare, I remember thinking that for her it was probably just then. Her long hair dividing over her bare shoulders, her lashes dark against her cheeks as she looked down at the page, she could go nowhere from this moment except away from it. She still had a long way to go before she left it for good, but I felt like Father Hopkins anyway as I watched her—

> How to keep . . . Back beauty, keep it, beauty, beauty,
> beauty, . . . from vanishing away?

" 'Expose thyself to feel what wretches feel,' she read, 'That thou may'st shake the superflux to them, And show the heavens more just' " and two, and *one* and two, the voice floated in through the open windows. Carl West had one hand up to his eyes as if to shield them from the sun, the other cupped at his crotch. The bee drifted heavily down from the ceiling and hit the blackboard with a little thud, then crawled drunkenly along the chalk tray.

I said, "Who are these poor naked wretches he's praying for, if she's right that he's praying?"

Greg Dixon said, "We are."

He said it to be funny—they were the poor naked wretches to have to sit there and listen to Laura Fleischman read blank verse when they could be off somewhere having whatever Greg Dixon thought of as

fun—but nobody laughed. Maybe I just ascribed my
own thoughts to them, but it seemed to me that for a
moment or two in that sleepy classroom they all felt
some unintended truth in Greg Dixon's words.

Laura Fleischman in the fullness of her time.
William Urquhart in his fatness. Greg Dixon with his
pimples. Carl West handsome and bored with the
knowledge that he could have any girl in that room.
They were the poor naked wretches, and at least for the
moment they knew they were. All of us. The "pitiless
storm"[2]

Out of the silence of a high-school classroom the tragic
word is spoken, and, if the teacher is right in his
conjectures, it is also heard. The poor naked wretches of the
world are all of them, everybody. They did not know it
before, but they know it now because they have heard it
spoken. Without the word, they might never have guessed
it, or, if they had guessed it, it would have been for them
only one more unspoken thing among many other unspoken
things that they carried around inside the worlds they were.
Once spoken, the word of their nakedness and wretchedness
is a shattering word. They are young and full of lunch and
full of hope and clothed in the beauty that it is to be young,
and thus of all people they are in a way the least naked, the
least wretched; but the word out of the old play tells them
for a moment otherwise. It speaks in a way they cannot
avoid hearing for themselves, which is the awesome power
of words because, although there are times when they shield
us from reality, at other times they assail us with it. The
play tells them that life is a pitiless storm and that they are
as vulnerable to it as Lear himself, not just in the sense that
youth grows old and beauty fades but in the sense that

youth and beauty themselves are vulnerable—their heads are houseless, their youth itself a looped and windowed raggedness and as inadequate to the task of sheltering them as their teacher's middle-aged urbanity is to the task of sheltering him. The word out of the play strips them for a moment naked and strips their teacher with them and to that extent Shakespeare turns preacher because stripping us naked is part of what preaching is all about, the tragic part.

To think of nakedness is to think of how we hide it from each other and ourselves, and suddenly there are all the Beecher lecturers again in all the clothes they wore. There were the nineteenth-century clothes in all their abundance—the long, full skirts and long sleeves and high collars, the shawls and scarves and gloves, the bonnets and stovepipe hats to keep out the weather—and there are our clothes, too, all of us wrapped up in our twentieth-century way and for our own reasons, to keep in, to keep out, whatever it is. The pitiless storm. There stand the lecturers clothed in all their clothes and clothed also in their accomplishments, their reputations for wit, eloquence, piety, churchmanship, knowledge, something, clothed in their pretensions, in the dignity that comes with being invited to lecture somewhere in the first place, clothed in the security of knowing that almost no matter what they said, people would assume they had said something worth listening to. Dean Inge was a flop, they tell us, serving up a lot of warmed-over scraps of this and that, but even as a flop he was Dean Inge still, clothed as unmistakably in Saint Paul's cathedral as in his hierarchical gaiters. And the people they lectured to, clothed in whatever they were clothed in and are clothed in still—their own securities and pretensions and reputations, their lecture-going expectations, their hope that maybe this time a word might be spoken to illumine not just their understanding but their lives, a life-giving word.

I speak of clothes not just as hypocrisy and disguise, though sometimes that for all of us, God knows, but of clothes as essential to survival because we cannot endure too much nakedness any more than we can endure too much silence, which strips us naked. And in *King Lear* too these images of clothes and nakedness abound as one of the recurring sets of images that keep the theme or word of the play as mobile and alive as the plot keeps the characters. Sometimes these images are verbal and sometimes they are made visible on the stage as in the scene where Lear exchanges his royal robes for rags and weeds to brave the storm in, where Edgar takes off his Saville Row tweeds to become instead a half-clothed Bedlam beggar, where the fool shivers in his flimsy motley against the cutting wind and Kent lays aside his ducal finery for a poor man's threadbare coveralls, cover-nothings. Even the wicked sisters, Goneril and Regan, though they retain to the end the gorgeous trappings of their rank, are in every other way denuded, exposed less for the wickedness than for the helplessness of what they are beneath.

Insofar as the word of the play is a tragic word, it rings out in its fullness when Lear comes upon Edgar standing half-naked on the bitter heath and asks for all of us, "Is man no more than this?" and then gives the answer to his own question. "Thou art the thing itself," Lear says. "Unaccommodated man is no more but such a poor, bare, forked animal as thou art" (3.4.105–11). Then the old king starts to tear off the few rags he has left as if in the awful lucidity of his madness he knows that if there is ever to be a true healing and helping, a true sheltering and clothing for any of us, it is with our nakedness and helplessness that it has to start. Almost the last thing he says as he is dying is

"Pray you, undo this button"(5.3.310), of all incongruous
and enchanted words, as if of all the moments of his life the
one he relives there at the end as most precious is the
moment when in his nakedness he was most kingly, when
in his helplessness he was most invincible, in the madness
of his despair most lucid. Shakespeare strips his characters
bare and, great preacher that he is, strips us bare along with
them as the high-school seniors were stripped in their
classroom. Beneath our clothes, our reputations, our
pretensions, beneath our religion or lack of it, we are all
vulnerable both to the storm without and to the storm
within, and if ever we are to find true shelter, it is with the
recognition of our tragic nakedness and need for true shelter
that we have to start. Thus it seems to me that this is also
where anyone who preaches the Gospel has to start too—
after the silence that is truth comes the news that is bad
before it is good, the word that is tragedy before it is
comedy because it strips us bare in order ultimately to
clothe us.

This is, of course, where Jesus starts, and his word of
tragedy is "Come unto me all ye who labor and are heavy
laden" and then stop there, stop there, because "I will give
you rest" is the word of comedy and comes later. *All ye who
labor and are heavy laden*—Jesus speaks his word as tragedian,
and the word floats free in the New Testament with no
special event to moor it to and no special listener pictured as
listening to it because it is addressed to anybody who will
listen, and there is no event to which it does not speak. It
floats loose so that it can find its mooring anywhere. When
he says, "Take up your cross and follow me," I think that
he is saying the same thing because before it means take up
some special mission or some special sacrifice or
responsibility, "take up your cross" means simply take up

the burden of your own life because for the time being anyway, maybe that is burden enough. Take it up in the sense of touch it and taste it and listen to it, look at yourself and your own life and smell the smell of your mortality and nakedness. All of you. Who are the poor naked wretches? Who are the ones that labor and are heavy laden? All ye, Jesus says—that is his tragic word to us, and his preachers must speak it after him if they are to be true to his truth.

There are all kinds of pressures on the preacher, both from within and without, to be all kinds of other things and to speak all kinds of other words. To speak the truth with love is to run the risk always of speaking only the truths that people love to hear you speak, and the preacher's temptation, among others, is to deal with those problems only to which there is, however complex and hard to arrive at, a solution. The pressure on the preacher is to be topical and contemporary, to speak out like the prophets against injustice and unrighteousness, and it is right that he should do so, crucial even, and if he does not goad to righteous action he fails both God and man. But he must remember the ones he is speaking to who beneath all the clothes they wear are the poor, bare, forked animals who labor and are heavy laden under the burden of their own lives let alone of the world's tragic life.

There is the one who can't stop thinking about suicide. The one who experiences his own sexuality as a guilt of which he can never be absolved. The one whose fear of death is only a screen behind which lies his deeper fear of life. The one who is in a way crippled by her own beauty because it has meant that she has never had to be loving or human to be loved but only beautiful. And the angry one. The lonely one. For the preacher to be relevant to the staggering problems of history is to risk being irrelevant to the staggering problems of the ones who sit there listening out of their own histories. To deal with the problems to which there is a possible solution can be a way of avoiding the problems to which humanly speaking there is no solution. When Jesus was brought to the place where his friend Lazarus lay dead, for instance, he did not offer any solution. He only wept. Then the other things he said and did. But first he simply let his tears be his word.

A young minister acquaintance of mine said not long ago, "There are two kinds of Christians in the world. There are gloomy Christians and there are joyful Christians," and there wasn't the shadow of a doubt which kind he preferred with his smile as bright as his clerical collar, full of bounce and zip and the gift of gab, and there is little doubt as to which we all prefer. And why not? Joy is at the end of it, after all. Astonishment and joy are what our faith finally points to, and even Saint Paul, that in a way gloomiest of Christians, said as much though he was hardly less battered than the Jesus he preached by the time he had come through his forty lashes less one, his stonings and shipwrecks and sleepless nights. Yet at the end, licking his wounds in a Roman lock-up, he wrote, "Rejoice in the Lord always. Again I will say, rejoice" (Phil. 4:4). But it is at the end that he wrote it. *Rejoice* is the last word and can be spoken only after the first word. The sheltering word can be spoken only after the word that leaves us without a roof over our heads, the answering word only after the word it answers.

The pressure on the preacher, of course, is to speak just the answer. The answer is what people have come to hear and what he has also come to hear, preaching always as much to himself as to anybody, to keep his spirits up. He has to give an answer because everybody else is giving answers. Transcendental meditation is an answer, and the Democratic party is an answer, or the Republican party, and acupuncture and acupressure are answers, and so are natural foods, yogurt, and brown rice. Yoga is an answer and transactional analysis and jogging. The pressure on the preacher is to promote the Gospel, to sell Christ as an answer that outshines all the other answers by talking up the shining side, by calling even the day of his death Good Friday when if it was good, it was good only after it was bad, the worst of all Fridays. The pressure is to be a public relations man, and why not, only not to the neglect of private relations, the relations especially of a man with God and with God less as a presence much of the time than as an absence, an empty place where grace and peace belong. The preacher has to be willing to speak as tragic a word as Jesus speaks, which is the word that even if all the problems that can be solved are solved—poverty, war, ignorance, injustice, disease—and even if all the answers the world can give are proved each in its own way workable, even so man labors and is heavy laden in his helplessness; poor naked wretch that bides the pelting of the storm that is no less pitiless for all the preaching of all the preachers.

When they brought Jesus to the place where his dead friend lay, Jesus wept. It is very easy to sentimentalize the scene and very tempting because to sentimentalize something is to look only at the emotion in it and at the emotion it stirs in us rather than at the reality of it, which we are always tempted not to look at because reality, truth, silence are all what we are not much good at and avoid when we can. To sentimentalize something is to savor rather than to suffer the sadness of it, is to sigh over the prettiness of it rather than to tremble at the beauty of it, which may make fearsome demands of us or pose fearsome threats. Not just as preachers but as Christians in general we are

particularly given to sentimentalizing our faith as much of
Christian art and Christian preaching bear witness—the
sermon as tearjerker, the Gospel an urn of long-stemmed
roses and baby's breath to brighten up the front of the
church, Jesus as Gregory Peck.

But here standing beside the dead body of his dead
friend he is not Gregory Peck. He has no form or comeliness
about him that we should desire him, and as one from
whom men hide their faces we turn from him. To see a man
weep is not a comely sight, especially this man whom we
want to be stronger and braver than a man, and the impulse
is to turn from him as we turn from anybody who weeps
because the sight of real tears, painful and disfiguring, forces
us to look to their source where we do not choose to look
because where his tears come from, our tears also come
from.

Why does he weep? The narrative tells us that the
people standing around him said that it was because he
loved Lazarus, and it is not hard to believe that that was
part of it. Lazarus is the only friend the Gospels name who
does not seem to have been a disciple especially but just a
friend, somebody he didn't have to be the messiah with
maybe but could just be himself with, somebody to have a
drink with once in a while, to tell what it was like to be
himself. Lazarus was his friend, and he loved him, so now
that he was dead, Jesus wept—wept for his friend and wept
for himself who would have to face the music from now on
without his friend. That is the way that some of the ones
who were there explained the tears they saw rolling down,
but others implied a different explanation, and we must
listen especially to them. They said, "Could not he who
opened the eyes of the blind man have kept this many from
dying?" (John 11:37).

It was a devastating thing to say because the chances

are that Jesus had already said it to himself. If he really was
the resurrection and the life, wasn't there something he
could have done to keep alive this one man's life? If God
was really in him, he and the Father one as he had said,
wasn't there something that God could have done? Both of
the dead man's sisters had said the same thing to him when
he first arrived. "Lord, if you had been here, my brother
would not have died" (John 11:21), Martha said, and a few
minutes later Mary also said it. The blunt fact of it was that
he had not been there, and their brother had died. The blunt
answer to the question, "Could not he who opened the eyes
of the blind man have kept this man from dying?" (John
11:37) was no. He could not. And there was something else
that was blunter still—that the God who was in him
apparently could not keep the man from dying either, or if
could not is not a verb that you can make God the subject of,
then *would not* or at least *did not*. The man died. Jesus wept.
And he wept not just out of love and loss, presumably, but
as one acquainted with a still deeper grief, which one can
imagine was grief both at his own failure to save the life of
Lazarus and also at the failure in some measure of his own
life and of the kingdom he preached, grief both at his own
absence when Lazarus needed him and at God's absence.

Later in the garden where it was his own death he had
to sweat out, we are told he sweated blood. He said,
"Father, if thou art willing, remove this cup from me" (Luke
22:42), and the cup was not removed from him presumably
because the Father was not willing to remove it, and one
suspects that the unwillingness of the Father may have been
harder for Jesus to choke down than the cup itself was.
Later it was harder still. By the time he had been hanging
there for a while, he had no tears left to weep with and no
more sweat, his tongue so dry he could hardly wrap it

around the words which are among the few he ever spoke
that people remembered in the language he spoke them in
probably because having once heard them, they could never
forget them no matter how hard they tried, and probably
they tried hard and often: "My God, my God, why have
you—" and then the Aramaic verb from an Arabic root
meaning to run out on, leave in the lurch, to be the Hell
and gone. "My God, my God, why hast thou forsaken me"
(Matt. 27:46). My God, where the Hell are you, meaning If
thou art our Father who art in Heaven, be thou also our
Father who art in Hell because Hell is where the action is,
where I am and the cross is. It is where the pitiless storm is.
It is where men labor and are heavy laden under the burden
of their own lives without you. Where they cut themselves
shaving and smoke three packs a day though they know the
surgeon general's warning by heart.

When the preacher climbs up into his pulpit, switches
on the lectern light and spreads out his note cards like a
poker hand, maybe even the vacationing sophomore who is
there only because somebody dragged him there pricks up
his ears for a second or two along with the rest of them
because they believe that the man who is standing up there
in a black gown with the little smear of styptic pencil on his
chin has something that they do not have or at least not in
the same way he has it because he is a professional. He
professes and stands for in public what they with varying
degrees of conviction or the lack of it subscribe to mainly in
private. He has been to a seminary and studied all that one
studies in a seminary. He has a degree to show for it, and
beyond the degree he has his ordination and the
extraordinary title of reverend, which no matter how well
they know him on the golf course or the cocktail-party

circuit sets him apart as one to be revered not because of
anything he knows or anything he is in himself but because,
as an ambassador is revered for the government he
represents, he is to be revered for representing Christ.

All of this deepens the silence with which they sit there
waiting for him to work a miracle, and the miracle they are
waiting for is that he will not just *say* that God is present,
because they have heard it said before and it has made no
great and lasting difference to them, will not just speak the
word of joy, hope, comedy, because they have heard it
spoken before too and have spoken it among themselves,
but that he will somehow make it real to them. They wait
for him to make God real to them through the sacrament of
words as God is supposed to become real in the sacrament
of bread and wine, and there is no place where the preacher
is more aware of his own nakedness and helplessness than
here in the pulpit as he listens to the silence of their
waiting. Poor, bare, forked animal in his cassock with his
heart in his mouth if not yet his foot. What can he say?
What word can he speak with power enough to empower
them, waiting there?

But let him take heart. He is called not to be an actor, a
magician, in the pulpit. He is called to be himself. He is
called to tell the truth as he has experienced it. He is called
to be human, to be human, and that is calling enough for
any man. If he does not make real to them the human
experience of what it is to cry into the storm and receive no
answer, to be sick at heart and find no healing, then he
becomes the only one there who seems not to have had that
experience because most surely under their bonnets and
shawls and jackets, under their afros and ponytails, all the
others there have had it whether they talk of it or not. As
much as anything else, it is their experience of the absence

of God that has brought them there in search of his presence, and if the preacher does not speak of that and to that, then he becomes like the captain of a ship who is the only one aboard who either does not know that the waves are twenty feet high and the decks awash or will not face up to it so that anything else he tries to say by way of hope and comfort and empowering becomes suspect on the basis of that one crucial ignorance or disingenuousness or cowardice or reluctance to speak in love any truths but the ones that people love to hear.

The absence of God is not just an idea to conjure with, an emptiness for the preacher to try to furnish, like a house, with chair and sofa, heat and light, to make it livable. The absence of God is just that which is not livable. It is the tears that Jesus wept over Lazarus and the sweat he sweated in the garden and the cry he choked out when his own tongue filled his mouth like a gag. The blackness of the preacher's black gown speaks of the anguish of it. The Bible he preaches out of speaks of it. The prophets and the psalms all speak of the one who is not there when he is most needed, not to mention Noah and Abraham, Gideon, Barak, Samson and David, and the rest of them who, if they did not speak of their anguish, carried it around in their hearts and grew whiskers and wore robes and armor and ephods and stovepipe hats to help conceal it even from themselves because, as the author of Hebrews strips them and all of us bare by putting it, "They all died without having received what was promised" (Heb. 11:13), the anguish of that, of having at most, and by no means every Sunday of the year, glimpsed it only from afar like a light on the horizon that could have been only moonshine.

The cross that is a symbol of defeat before it is a symbol of victory speaks also of the absence of God, and

Jesus speaks of it. He says, "Seeing they do not see and
hearing they do not hear" (Matt. 13:13). He says, "Why
does this generation seek a sign? Truly I say to you, no sign
will be given to this generation" (Matt. 12:39), and on the
cross as far as we are told no sign was given to him either,
just a sponge soaked in Dago red and a word of cold
comfort from the good thief who asked to be remembered in
his kingly power, asked him who died without the power to
raise spit and looked less like a king than like a street
accident. He says. "My God, my God, why have you left me
holding the bag, holding the world, when I can hardly any
longer hold up my own head?"

Jesus shares with us the darkness of what it is to be
without God as well as showing forth the glory of what it is
to be with God. He speaks about it, and perhaps that is
much of why, although we have not followed him very well
these past two thousand years or so, we have never quite
been able to stop listening to him. We listen almost in spite
of ourselves when he tells us the ship is sinking with all
hands aboard. All of you labor and are heavy laden, he says.
It is an appalling thing to tell us when we are trying so hard
to pretend that it is not so, just as it is appalling to tell even
the young and beautiful and full of hope that the poor
naked wretches of the world are themselves. But even as we
are appalled, we listen because we know that he knows the
worst as well as we do. Kilroy has been there before us.

The old ones and the young one. The smart ones and
the dumb ones. The lucky and the unlucky. The eggheads
and potheads, the Gay Libs and Hard Hats. They all listen
as they may listen even to the preacher if he will take the
chance himself of being embarrassing, appalling us by
exposing the nakedness of the poor naked wretches and his
own nakedness. The world hides God from us, or we hide

ourselves from God, or for reasons of his own God hides
himself from us, but however you account for it, he is often
more conspicuous by his absence than by his presence, and
his absence is much of what we labor under and are heavy
laden by. Just as sacramental theology speaks of a doctrine
of the Real Presence, maybe it should speak also of a
doctrine of the Real Absence because absence can be
sacramental, too, a door left open, a chamber of the heart
kept ready and waiting.

It is out of the whirlwind that Job first hears God say
"Who is this that darkens counsel by words without
knowledge" (Job 42:3). It is out of the absence of God that
God makes himself present, and it is not just the whirlwind
that stands for his absence, not just the storm and chaos of
the world that knocks into a cocked hat all man's attempts
to find God in the world, but God is absent also from all
Job's words about God, and from the words of his
comforters, because they are words without knowledge that
obscure the issue of God by trying to define him as present
in ways and places where he is not present, to define him as
moral order, as the best answer man can give to the problem
of his life. God is not an answer man can give, God says.
God himself does not give answers. He gives himself, and
into the midst of the whirlwind of his absence gives himself.

There is also Elijah. Jezebel, the queen, dynamites the
holy places and guns down the prophets until Elijah is the
only one left with no more reason to believe that God will
intervene on his behalf than he did on behalf of the others.
So he hides out in the wilderness, and once again there is
the great storm to whose blast Elijah is as naked as the rest
of them, and God is not present in the storm, not in the
wind or the earthquake or the fire, and it is his not being
present that makes the storm unendurable or that *is* the

storm because the eye of the storm is God's eye, the stillness
and emptiness at the center of the storm is the voice he
speaks with, the still, small voice you have to strain to hear.
It is the same storm that Lear rages against, of course, with
his "Blow, winds, and crack your cheeks! rage! blow! / You
cataracts and hurricanoes, spout" (3.2.1–2). It is enough to
drive a man mad as Lear and the prophets were all mad.
Both the inner world and the outer world are threatened
beyond enduring.

There would be a strong argument for saying that much
of the most powerful preaching of our time is the preaching
of the poets, playwrights, novelists because it is often they
better than the rest of us who speak with awful honesty
about the absence of God in the world and about the storm
of his absence, both without and within, which, because it is
unendurable, unlivable, drives us to look to the eye of the
storm. I think of *King Lear* especially with its tragic vision of
a world in which the good and the bad alike go down to
dusty and, it would seem, equally meaningless death with
no God to intervene on their behalf, and yet with its vision
of a world in which the naked and helpless ones, the victims
and fools, become at least truly alive before they die and
thus touch however briefly on something that lies beyond
the power of death. It is the worldly ones, the ones wise as
the world understands wisdom and strong in the way the
world understands strength, who are utterly doomed. This is
so much the central paradox of *Lear* that the whole play can
be read as a gloss if not a homily on that passage in First
Corinthians where Paul expresses the same paradox in
almost the same terms by writing, "God chose what is
foolish in the world to shame the wise. God chose what is
weak in the world to shame the strong. God chose what is
low and despised in the world, even things that are not, to

bring to nothing things that are" (1 Cor. 1:27–28), thus
pointing as Shakespeare points to the apparent emptiness of
the world where God belongs and to how the emptiness
starts to echo like an empty shell after a while until you can
hear in it the still, small voice of the sea, hear strength in
weakness, victory in defeat, presence in absence.

I think of Dostoevski in *The Brothers Karamazov* when the
body of Alyosha's beloved Father Zossima begins to stink in
death instead of giving off fragrance as the dead body of a
saint is supposed to, and at the very moment where Alyosha
sees the world most abandoned by God, he suddenly finds
the world so aflame with God that he rushes out of the
chapel where the body lies and kisses the earth as the
shaggy face of the world where God, in spite of and in the
midst of everything, is. I think of Herman Melville's *Moby
Dick* where in his sermon on the Book of Jonah Father
Mapple charges all preachers not to shrink from facing for
themselves and proclaiming the dark side of truth as
Alyosha was forced by the stench of death to face it by
saying:

> Woe to him whom this world charms from Gospel duty.
> Woe to him who seeks to pour oil upon the waters
> when God has brewed them into a gale. Woe to him
> who seeks to please rather than to appal. Woe to him
> whose good name is more to him than goodness. Woe
> to him who, in this world, courts not dishonor! Woe to
> him who would not be true, even though to be false
> were salvation. Yea, woe to him who, as the great Pilot
> Paul has it, while preaching to others is himself a
> castaway.[3]

Melville himself as preacher appals us by speaking the
tragic truth of a dark and storm-tossed world where even
the whiteness of the great white whale is ambiguous,

standing on the one hand for beauty, gladness, holiness, the priests's white vestments at Passiontide, and, on the other hand, for the whiteness of sharks and snowbound wilderness and death—"Not so much a color," he writes, "as the visible absence of color . . . a colorless, all-color of atheism from which we shrink."[4]

The absence is visible, Melville says—we can see it— but if atheism is one of the things we see in it and shrink from, the temptation not to believe, there is something else to see in it as well, and this is what the Jesuit poet Gerard Manley Hopkins writes of in his great poem about the sinking of the sailing ship *Deutschland* in a winter storm off the coast of England with the exiled Franciscan nuns aboard. He pictures the storm itself, this same storm. He pictures the black-backed, widow-making, unchilding, unfathering deeps as he calls it, the bitter wind driving the snow and the murderous breakers before it, and then he says,

> Be adored among men,
> God, . . .
> Wring thy rebel, . . .
> . . . with wrecking and storm.
> Beyond saying sweet, past telling of tongue,
> Thou art lightning and love, I found it, a winter and warm.
> Father and fondler of heart thou hast wrung:
> Hast thy dark descending and art most merciful then.[5]
>
> [Stanza 9]

In the fury of the storm he sees what he calls "past all / Grasp God, throned behind / Death with a sovereignty that heeds but hides, bodes but abides / With a mercy that outrides / The all of water, an ark / For the listener; for the lingerer with a love glides / Lower than death and the dark" (Stanzas 32–33). It is to this past-all-grasp God who heeds

but hides and is throned lower and more ultimate than
death and dark that the tall nun calls out, "O Christ come
quickly" (Stanza 24) until finally he comes and grasps her in
the midst of the storm, "Not a dooms-day dazzle in his
coming nor dark as he came; / Kind, but royally reclaiming
his own" (Stanza 34), so that at the end of the poem this
poet, than whom no Christian ever saw deeper into the
dark, can call out for all of us, "Let him easter in us, be a
dayspring to the dimness of us, be a crimson-cresseted east"
(Stanza 35). For Hopkins, as for the others, to speak the
truth with power meant to be true to the experience of truth
as among other things stormbound and tragic.

"In the beginning . . . the earth was without form and
void, and darkness was upon the face of the deep," (Gen.
1:1–2), and as in the beginning so also now because there is
never a time when darkness and dimness are not upon the
face of the deep and upon our own faces. What gives such
power to the preaching of these artists and what makes
them voices that all preachers would do well to learn from is
that they are willing to appall and bless us with their tragic
word—to speak out of the darkness and weep as Jesus wept
because maybe only then can the reality of the other word
become real to us, the word which to the darkness upon the
face of the deep is "God said let there be light, and there
was light" (Gen. 1:3), which to all those who labor and are
heavy laden is "and I will give you rest." They preach the
word of human tragedy, of a world where men can at best
see God only dimly and from afar, because it is truth and
because it is a word which must be spoken as prelude if the
other word is to become sacramental and real, too, which is
the word that God has overcome the dark world—the word
of divine comedy.

III . . . The Gospel as Comedy

THE place to start is with a woman laughing. She is an old woman, and, after a lifetime in the desert, her face is cracked and rutted like a six-month drought. She hunches her shoulders around her ears and starts to shake. She squinnies her eyes shut, and her laughter is all China teeth and wheeze and tears running down as she rocks back and forth in her kitchen chair. She is laughing because she is pushing ninety-one hard and has just been told she is going to have a baby. Even though it was an angel who told her, she can't control herself, and her husband can't control himself either. He keeps a straight face a few seconds longer than she does, but he ends by cracking up, too. Even the angel is not unaffected. He hides his mouth behind his golden scapular, but you can still see his eyes. They are larkspur blue and brimming with something of which the laughter of the old woman and her husband is at best only a rough translation.

The old woman's name is Sarah, of course, and the old man's name is Abraham, and they are laughing at the idea of a baby's being born in the geriatric ward and Medicare's picking up the tab. They are laughing because the angel not only seems to believe it but seems to expect them to believe it too. They are laughing because with part of themselves they do believe it. They are laughing because with another part of themselves they know it would take a fool to believe it. They are laughing because laughing is better than crying and maybe not even all that different. They are laughing because if by some crazy chance it should just happen to come true, then they would really have something to laugh about. They are laughing at God and with God, and they are laughing at themselves too because laughter has that in common with weeping. No matter what the immediate occasion is of either your laughter or your tears, the object of both ends up being yourself and your own life.

They had had quite a life, the old pair. Years before, they had gotten off to a good start in Mesopotamia. They had a nice house in the suburbs with a two-car garage and color TV and a barbecue pit. They had a room all fixed up for when the babies started coming. With their health and each other and their families behind them they had what is known as a future. Sarah got her clothes at Bonwit's, did volunteer work at the hospital, was a member of the League of Women Voters. Abraham was pulling down an excellent salary for a young man, plus generous fringe benefits and an enlightened retirement plan. And then they got religion, or religion got them, and Abraham was convinced that what God wanted them to do was pull up stakes and head out for Canaan where God had promised that he would make

Abraham the father of a great nation which would in turn
be a blessing to all nations, so that's what they did, and
that's where their troubles started.

They put the house on the market and gave the color
TV to the hospital and got a good price for the crib and the
bassinet because they had never been used and were good as
new. Abraham wrote an eloquent letter of resignation to the
president of the company and received an equally eloquent
one in reply, assuring him that there would always be a job
waiting for him if he ever changed his mind and came back.
"If he ever regained his senses and came back" was the way
the president expressed it in his first draft because though
he thought religion was a good thing, like social security
and regular exercise, he didn't think it was something to go
overboard about like Abraham, but in his final draft he
settled for the milder wording.

So off they went in their station wagon with a U-haul
behind and a handful of friends and relations who, if they
didn't share Abraham's religious convictions, decided to
hitch their wagons to his star anyway. Among the people
they took was their brother-in-law Lot. It turned out to be a
bad mistake.

The Yiddish word *schlemiel* has been translated as the
kind of person who is always going around spilling soup on
people and a *schlemozzle* as the kind of person he is always
spilling it on, and by that definition Abraham was a
schlemozzle. The first thing that went wrong on their journey
took place when the Egyptian pharaoh was struck by Sarah's
beauty and made a serious play for her. Abraham, fearing
that if Pharaoh discovered that she was a married woman he
might decide to get rid of her husband, advised her to say
she was his sister instead of his wife and let the chips fall
where they might. This led to a complicated domestic

situation which almost cost Abraham the woman who was to be the mother of the great nation and from which he was finally able to extricate himself only by admitting he'd lied and thereby sustaining a considerable loss both of face and of credibility.

The next thing that went wrong took place when they finally limped into the promised land and a nasty situation developed between Abraham and his in-laws. Lot and his crowd claimed that the place wasn't big enough for both of them, and Abraham's crowd said they couldn't agree more, so, as a way out of the impasse, Abraham proposed that they divide the land in two and each take half. He then made the mistake of telling Lot that he could have first choice, and of course Lot chose the half that was fertile pastureland around the Jordan River and Abraham was left with the disaster area around Dead Man's Gulch. In other words, all of Canaan was the Promised Land, but some parts were more promising than others.

The next thing was the worst. Chosen by God Himself to be the prospective father of a great nation, Abraham made the discovery that he didn't stand a Chinaman's chance of becoming the father of anything because after extensive medical examinations all the leading authorities agreed that Sarah was as barren as most of the real estate Lot had stuck them with.

So the years rolled by like empty perambulators until finally when Abraham was one hundred and Sarah was ninety, the angel arrived to make his shattering announcement. He said that when God made a promise, he stuck to it, and Sarah was going to have a boy. Then they laughed. One account says that Abraham laughed until he fell on his face, and the other account says that Sarah was the one who did it. She was hiding behind the door of their tent when the angel spoke, and it was her laughter that got

them all going. According to Genesis, God intervened then
and asked about Sarah's laughter, and Sarah was scared stiff
and denied the whole thing. Then God said, "No, but you
did laugh," and, of course, he was right. Maybe the most
interesting part of it all is that far from getting angry at
them for laughing, God told them that when the baby was
born he wanted them to name him Isaac, which in Hebrew
means laughter. So you can say that God not only tolerated
their laughter but blessed it and in a sense joined in it
himself, which makes it a very special laughter indeed—God
and man laughing together, sharing a glorious joke in which
both of them are involved. It is perhaps as important to look
closely into the laughter of Abraham and Sarah as it is
important to look closely into the tears of Jesus.

When Jesus wept over the dead body of his friend
Lazarus, many things seem to have been at work in him,
and there seem to have been many levels to his grief. He
wept because his friend was dead and he had loved him.
Beneath that he wept because, as Mary and Martha both
tactlessly reminded him, if he had only been present,
Lazarus needn't have died, and he was not present. Beneath
that, he wept perhaps because if only God had been present,
then too Lazarus needn't have died, and God was not
present either, at least not in the way and to the degree that
he was needed. Then, beneath even that, it is as if his grief
goes so deep that it is for the whole world that Jesus is
weeping and the tragedy of the human condition, which is
to live in a world where again and again God is not present,
at least not in the way and to the degree that man needs
him. Jesus sheds his tears at the visible absence of God in
the world where the good and bad alike go down to defeat
and death. He sheds his tears at the audible silence of God
at those moments especially when a word from him would
mean the difference between life and death, or at the

deafness of men which prevents their hearing him, the blindness of men which prevents even Jesus himself as a man from seeing him to the extent that at the moment of all moments when he needs him most he cries out his Eloi Eloi, which is a cry so dark that of the four evangelists, only two of them have the stomach to record it as the last word he spoke while he still had a human mouth to speak with. Jesus wept, we all weep, because even when man is good, even when he is Jesus, God makes himself scarce for reasons that no theodicy has ever fathomed.

One thinks of Stephen Crane's little poem

> A man said to the universe:
> "Sir, I exist!"
> "However," replied the universe,
> "The fact has not created in me
> A sense of obligation."[6]

One thinks of Albert Camus with his doctrine of the Absurd as the coming together of man's insatiable longing for life to make sense and life's inexorable refusal to do so. One thinks of Jean Paul Sartre's thesis that even if God existed, it would make no difference to his view of man as condemned to forge his own destiny in terrible freedom because God might as well not exist for all he shows of himself. One thinks of Gerard Manley Hopkins:

> Thou art indeed just, Lord, if I contend
> With thee; but, sir, so what I plead is just.
> Why do sinners' ways prosper? and why must
> Disappointment all I endeavour end?
> Wert thou my enemy, O thou, my friend,
> How wouldst thou worse, I wonder, than thou dost
> Defeat, thwart me? . . .[7]

[#74]

One thinks of King Lear and how he achieves through his suffering a kind of Olympian and beatific vision of the tragic beauty and majesty of things only to die a pathetic old man, holding a feather to Cordelia's lips and babbling that his darling is still alive when everybody can see she lies there cold and dead as a haddock. And finally, or firstly, one thinks of ourselves, who do not need to be poets or philosophers or kings or Christs to know these things too if we will speak what we feel and not what we ought to say. As much as it is our hope, it is our hopelessness that brings us to church of a Sunday, and any preacher who, whatever else he speaks, does not speak to that hoplessness might as well save his breath.

Then a strange and unexpected sound is heard. It is like the creaking of a rusty hinge. It is like ice starting to crack up in a pond in March. It is like the sound of hens cackling, of the old Ford trying to turn over on a winter morning. It is the sound of laughter, of an old woman and an old man knocking themselves out in a tent. It starts out dry and small and ends so uproarious and big that to preserve his dignity even the angel has to turn his face aside.

Before we ask any questions about it, we should first just listen to it. It starts with a startled catch of the breath because the last thing either of them expected to do was to laugh, and it takes them by surprise as much as it takes us. It wells up in their throats like sorrow, only it is not sorrow, and contorts their old faces like tears, only that's not what it is either, or at least a different kind of tears. Their shoulders shake. Their faces go red. Their China teeth slip a notch. She will be ninety-one on her next birthday, and the angel says she will celebrate it in the maternity ward. Sarah stuffs her apron to her mouth. Abraham gasps for air.

Then the question: Where does their laughter come

from? It comes from as deep a place as tears come from, and in a way it comes from the same place. As much as tears do, it comes out of the darkness of the world where God is of all missing persons the most missed, except that it comes not as an ally of darkness but as its adversary, not as a symptom of darkness but as its antidote. The laughter of Abraham and Sarah at the angel's extraordinary announcment does not eliminate the darkness, because through the long, childless years of the past, darkness has already taken its toll, and in the long years that lie ahead there will be darkness for them still as, for instance, when Abraham is asked to take the child of the promise and offer him to God as a burnt offering. They both still have to face the darkness both of death and of life in a world where God is seen at best only from afar, through a glass darkly; but with their laughter something new breaks into their darkness, something so unexpected and preposterous and glad that they can only laugh at it in astonishment.

To weep at tragedy as Jesus wept is to weep at that which is inevitable. Given the vulnerability of man and the pitiless storm of the world, tragedy is bound to happen. Given the sinfulness of man and the temptation of the world to sin, tragedy is bound to happen. Man is born to trouble as the sparks fly upward, Job says, and there is an inevitability to the tears we shed over it. They are part of what it means to be human. But the announcement of the angel is just the reverse of that.

They are going to have a baby after all. It is just what was bound not to happen. The old *schlemozzle* is going to be the father of a great nation in spite of everything. It is just what was not inevitable. If anything was inevitable, it was that the soup would be spilled on him again. The stranger who appeared at their tent door turned out to be not a man to read the meter but an angel. Who could have possibly predicted it? Who could have possibly made it happen, grabbed an angel by the wing and pulled him down out of the sky and contrived for him to give such astonishing news? It all happened not of necessity, not inevitably, but gratuitously, freely, hilariously. And what was astonishing, gratuitous, hilarious was, of course, the grace of God. What could they do but laugh at the preposterousness of it, and they laughed until the tears ran down their cheeks.

The tragic is the inevitable. The comic is the unforeseeable. How can Donald Duck foresee that after being run over by a steamroller he will pick himself up on the other side as flat as a pancake for a few seconds but alive and squawking? How can Charlie Chaplin in his baggy pants and derby hat foresee that though he is stood up by the girl and clobbered over the head by the policeman and hit in the kisser with a custard pie, he will emerge dapper and gallant to the end, twirling his invincible cane and twitching his invincible moustache? Bored to death by his comforters and scratching his boils and facing the undertaker's unpaid bill for the multiple funeral of his children and entire household staff, how could Job possibly foresee that his bloodshot eyes would indeed behold, and by no means as a stranger, the one who laid the foundations of the earth and at whose work the morning stars sang together and all the sons of God shouted for joy? Who could have predicted that God would choose not Esau, the honest and reliable, but Jacob, the trickster and heel, that he would put the finger on Noah, who hit the bottle, or on Moses, who was trying to beat the rap in Midian for braining a man in Egypt and said if it weren't for the honor of the thing he'd just as soon let Aaron go back and face the music, or on the prophets, who were a ragged lot, mad as hatters most of them and dragging their heels to a man when they were called to hit the sawdust trail? Who could have foretold that out of the sordid affair between David and Uriah's wife, Bethsheba, Solomon would be born with his high IQ and his passion for ecclesiastical architecture and that out of Solomon would be born a whole line of apostate kings ending finally in a king the likes of whom nobody could possibly have foretold except maybe Second Isaiah, who saw at least that it wasn't his *beaux yeux* that would draw men to him or by the power of his heavy artillery that he would king it over them?

And, of course, there is the comedy, the unforeseeableness, of the election itself. Of all the peoples he could have chosen to be his holy people, he chose the Jews, who as somebody has said are just like everybody else only more so—more religious than anybody when they were religious and when they were secular, being secular as if they'd invented it. And the comedy of the covenant—God saying "I will be your God and you shall be my people" (Exod. 6:7) to a people who before the words had stopped ringing in their ears were dancing around the golden calf like aborigines and carrying on with every agricultural deity and fertility god that came down the pike. And yet it was this people who produced, as their greatest king but one, a king who danced another dance altogether: David the king stripping himself down to his fig leaf and to the unmixed horror of his aristocratic wife dancing like a madman before the ark of the Lord because more than most he got the wonderful joke of it. The comedy of grace as what needn't happen and can't possibly happen because it can only impossibly happen and happens in the dark that only just barely fails to swallow it up.

Jesus says, "Come unto me all you who labor and are

heavy laden" (Matt. 11:28). That is the tragedy. Our
laboring couldn't have been otherwise, given who we are
and who we are not, given who God is and who he is not,
given this world in all its beauty and pain to live in and die
in. Then he says, "And I will give you rest" (Matt. 11:28).
That is the comedy, and the comedy has to do with both
Jesus as the speaker and the Gospel word he speaks.

Paul was the first one who dared come out with it
when he wrote the church at Corinth about the folly of the
Gospel and said, "We preach Christ crucified, a stumbling
block to Jews and a folly" (1Cor. 1:23) to everybody else,
the comedy of what we preach, in other words: Christ's
whole life a kind of comedy. When Christ was born in the
darkness of the night, the sky was lit by a multitude of the
heavenly host singing him into life with their great hymn.
But even the ones who knew about it, even his own mother
and brother, seem to have forgotten it soon enough so that
when he came to Nazareth sounding like a Messiah, they
thought he'd gone off the deep end and started to throw
him off the edge of a cliff to demonstrate their point
graphically. He galvanized thousands with his miracles—
healing and casting out demons and feeding a whole
ballpark with his five loaves and two fish—but, like Chinese
food, the miracles didn't stick to their ribs so that he might
as well have saved his strength for all the lasting good they
did. He spoke in words that nobody much seems to have
understood, least of all the disciples, and when he spoke of
the necessity of his death, even Peter told him he was going
too far. At the last meal he ever ate with his friends when
the goon squad was already laying for him in the shadows
and all Hell was about to break loose, the great confidence
with which he says, "Be of good cheer, I have overcome the
world" (John 16:33) becomes the great confidence of Charlie

Chaplin as the little tramp standing there so jaunty and
hopeful in his baggy pants and derby hat while the whole
world he has overcome threatens to crash down on him like
a pail of water balanced on the top of a door. When finally
they string him up, they do it for the wrong reasons and
string him up as a nationalist revolutionary when the only
revolution he is after is a revolution of the human heart and
his concern is ultimately for all nations. Even the
resurrection has a kind of comedy to it. His closest followers
dismiss it out of hand at first as an old wives' tale, and
when Mary Magdalen comes upon him in the dim halflight
of dawn, she mistakes him for the gardner of all people. The
red marks on his hands are where he is holding roses. The
trouble he is having with his feet comes from miles of
patroling the gravel walks to pick up gum wrappers with a
pointed stick.

    "A stumbling block to the Jews and folly to the
Gentiles" (1Cor. 1:23), Paul writes, because it is truth. The
folly of preaching Christ crucified, preaching the king who
looks like a tramp, the prince of peace who looks like the
prince of fools, the lamb of God who ends like something
hung up at the butcher's. Dostoevski echoes this when he
writes a novel about Christ as a Russian prince and calls it
The Idiot. The painter Rouault echoes it when he paints
Christ as a clown. The musical *Godspell* echoes it by rigging
him out as if for a three-ring circus in white-face and
acrobat's tights. The theologian Kierkegaard echoes it by
ringing endless changes on the words "Come unto me all
you who labor and are heavy laden and I will give you rest"
as the words of the lowly and helpless one who would seem
to have least to offer being at the same time the high and
mighty one who crazily claims to have most to offer.

    The comedy of all this is not the black comedy it might

at first seem to Jew and Gentile alike, who have learned of
the world to see all things as black at last, but white
comedy, high comedy, the high comedy of Christ that is as
close to tears as the high comedy of Buster Keaton or
Marcel Marceau or Edith Bunker is close to tears—but glad
tears at last, not sad tears, tears at the hilarious
unexpectedness of things rather than at their tragic
expectedness.

There are even times when Jesus seems to see the
comedy of his own life. His fellow Nazarenes, the ones he
grew up with, worked with, played with, come at him with
fire in their eyes to throw him off the cliff as a blasphemer
at worst and a lunatic at best, and he says to them
"Doubtless you will quote to me this proverb, 'Physician
heal yourself' " (Luke 4:23). He sees how they see the
preposterousness of Jesus, the carpenter's son, putting
himself forth as Christ, God's son. He sees how they are
affronted by him as one who proclaims himself anointed to
preach the good news to the poor when it is no news to
anybody that he is himself the poorest of all. He says, "The
blind receive their sight, the lame walk, the deaf hear, the
dead are raised up . . . / and blessed is he who takes no
offense at me" (Matt. 11:5–6) which is to say blessed is he
who sees that, all appearances to the contrary
notwithstanding, he is who he says he is and does what he
says he does if they will only, at admittedly great cost to
their pride, their common sense, their sad vision of what is
and is not possible in the stormy world, let him do it.
Blessed is he, in other words, who gets the joke.

Apart from the comedy of Jesus himself, there is also
the comedy of the word he speaks and the form in which he
speaks it, which is most characteristically the form of the
parable. "He said nothing without a parable" (Matt. 13:13).

Matthew tells us, and Mark tells us the same thing. Unlike
the prophets, Jesus has little to say about the international
situation and the role of Israel as a nation among nations.
Except by inference he has little to say about the specific
historical problems of his day such as poverty, slavery,
social injustice, the ambiguities of a semiautonomous Jewish
theocracy trying to survive under the comparatively
benevolent despotism of the secular Roman state. In this
sense he is not, as a preacher, a Jeremiah or a Martin
Niemöller or a Reinhold Niebuhr, relating religious faith to
the great public issues of his time, or if he was, these are
not the words he spoke that have mainly come down to us.
It was not the great public issues that Jesus traded in but
the great private issues, not the struggles of the world
without but the struggles of the world within. When
Matthew tries to account for the way Jesus preached, he
quotes from the Seventy-Eighth Psalm, "I will open my
mouth in parables, I will utter what has been hidden since
the foundations of the world" (Matt. 13:35), and insofar as
it was the hidden and private and ultimately inexpressible
that Jesus preached about, in a sense he had no recourse but
to preach in the way he did, not in the incendiary rhetoric
of the prophet or the systematic abstractions of the
theologian but in the language of images and metaphor,
which is finally the only language you can use if you want
not just to elucidate the hidden thing but to make it come
alive.

What is the kingdom of God? He does not speak of a
reorganization of society as a political possibility or of the
doctrine of salvation as a doctrine. He speaks of what it is
like to find a diamond ring that you thought you'd lost
forever. He speaks of what it is like to win the Irish
Sweepstakes. He suggests rather than spells out. He evokes

rather than explains. He catches by surprise. He doesn't let the homiletic seams show. He is sometimes cryptic, sometimes obscure, sometimes irreverent, always provocative. He tells stories. He speaks in parables, and though we have approached these parables reverentially all these many years and have heard them expounded as grave and reverent vehicles of holy truth, I suspect that many if not all of them were originally not grave at all but were antic, comic, often more than just a little shocking. I suspect that Jesus spoke many of his parables as a kind of sad and holy joke and that that may be part of why he seemed reluctant to explain them because if you have to explain a joke, you might as well save your breath. I don't mean jokes for the joke's sake, of course. I don't mean the kind of godly jest the preacher starts his sermon with to warm people up and show them that despite his Geneva tabs or cassock he can laugh with the rest of them and is as human as everybody else. I mean the kind of joke Jesus told when he said it is harder for a rich person to enter Paradise than for a Mercedes to get through a revolving door, harder for a rich person to enter Paradise than for Nelson Rockefeller to get through the night deposit slot of the First National City Bank. And then added that though for man it is impossible, for God all things are possible because God is the master of the impossible, and he is a master of the impossible because in terms of what man thinks possible he is in the end a wild and impossible god. It seems to me that more often than not the parables can be read as high and holy jokes about God and about man and about the Gospel itself as the highest and holiest joke of them all.

Who is the God man prays to out of his fathomless need—"Wert thou my enemy, O thou my friend, how wouldst thou worse, I wonder, defeat, thwart me?"[8] One has only to think of the images that come first to our own minds to realize the special quality of the images that Jesus uses. We might say God is like the great physician with a cure for every ill. He is like the good president whose Oval Office is always open to even the humblest citizen. But Jesus says something quite different. He says God is like a man who, when his friend comes knocking at his door at midnight, says, "You'll wake the children. Drop dead," and who only after his friend goes on leaning on the doorbell finally staggers downstairs with his hair in his eyes and his bathrobe on inside out and gives him what he wants just to be shot of him. Jesus says God is like the crooked lawyer with the book he is writing about his involvement in Watergate so much on his mind that he couldn't care less whether the woman wins her suit against the power company but finally tells his secretary to show her in anyway just so she won't keep bugging him. Does God answer the prayers of man? Jesus says if your ten year old asks you for a goldfish, do you give him a black widow spider? If he comes to you for an Eskimo Pie, do you knock out his two front teeth? It is almost as if he is saying a foolish question deserves a foolish answer. The foolishness of what we preach.

Elsewhere, as Jesus tells it, the comedy about God deepens and becomes even more antic and unexpected, which would seem to be part of what comedy is all about. The parable of the talents, for instance. The five-talent man puts his five talents on Beautiful Dreamer to come in first in the fifth at Saratoga and doubles his money. The two-talent man gets his broker to buy him two shares of United Distillers and when the market goes up does as well as the five-talent man. The one-talent man, on the other hand, plays it safe and with good reason. As he explains it later,

he knows that his benefactor is a hard man, and in terms of
the way things turn out for him, he is dead right. So when
the one-talent man gets his one talent, he's scared out of his
wits he may lose it and, instead of shooting for the moon,
stuffs it in an old sock and shoots it up the chimney. Then,
as hearers of the parable, we wait for the punch line we
think we see coming. The benefactor will say, "Play it safe
like the one talent man. Don't play the ponies. God is a
hard God. Treasure what he gives you so you'll be sure you
still have it the next time he checks you out." Only of
course that's just what the benefactor doesn't say, as Jesus
tells it. It is the all-or-nothing ones who are held up as
shining examples of what it is to have faith, to have life, to
have courage or whatever it is it takes, and the
better-be-safe-than-be-sorry one who gets it in the neck for
taking the faith or life or courage or whatever it is he's been
given and tucking it under his tail and sitting on it like an
old grad on a hot water bottle at the fifty-yard line on a
chilly October Saturday.

   "From him who has much it will be taken and given to
him who has little?" That is what we might expect. But it is
not what we get. Instead "To him who has, more will be
given" (Matt. 13:12), Jesus has the benefactor preposterously
say, "and from him who has not even what he has will be
taken away" because that is truth and because if the parable
is comedy, it is high comedy and the tears it is close to are
in this case tears for the one-talent man who heads off for
outer darkness with his hot-water bottle under his arm
because that is what life comes to for the half alive. Except I
wonder if part of what the unexpectedness and comedy of
the parable may suggest is that even the one-talent man's
tragedy points to a joke still farther in and deeper down,
which is that since for God all things are possible, even the

one-talent man will be impossibly saved in the end just as
the camel somehow impossibly makes it through the eye of
the needle in the end.

God is the comic shepherd who gets more of a kick out
of that one lost sheep once he finds it again than out of the
ninety and nine who had the good sense not to get lost in
the first place. God is the eccentric host who, when the
country-club crowd all turn out to have other things more
important to do than come live it up with him, goes out into
the skid rows and soup kitchens and charity wards and
brings home a freak show. The man with no legs who sells
shoelaces at the corner. The old woman in the moth-eaten
fur coat who makes her daily rounds of the garbage cans.
The old wino with his pint in a brown paper bag. The
pusher, the whore, the village idiot who stands at the
blinker light waving his hand as the cars go by. They are
seated at the damask-laid table in the great hall. The candles
are all lit and the champagne glasses filled. At a sign from
the host, the musicians in their gallery strike up *"Amazing
Grace."* If you have to explain it, don't bother.

I think that these parables can be read as jokes about
God in the sense that what they are essentially about is the
outlandishness of God who does impossible things with
impossible people, and I believe that the comedy of them is
not just a device for making the truth that they contain go
down easy but that the truth that they contain can itself be
thought of as comic. It is hard to think of any place where
this is more apparent than in the greatest parable of them
all, the one that is in its own way both the most comic and
the most sad. The Prodigal Son goes off with his inheritance
and blows the whole pile on liquor and sex and fancy
clothes until finally he doesn't have two cents left to rub
together and has to go to work or starve to death. He gets a

job on a pig farm and keeps at it long enough to observe
that the pigs are getting a better deal than he is and then
decides to go home. There is nothing edifying about his
decision. There is no indication that he realizes he's made an
ass of himself and broken his old man's heart, no indication
that he thinks of his old man as anything more than a meal
ticket. There is no sign that he is sorry for what he's done
or that he's resolved to make amends somehow and do
better next time. He decides to go home for the simple
reason that he knows he always got three squares a day at
home, and for a man who is in danger of starving to death,
that is reason enough. So he sets out on the return trip and
on the way rehearses the speech he hopes will soften the
old man's heart enough so that at least he won't slam the
door in his face. "Father, I have sinned against heaven and
against you. I am no longer worthy to be called your son."
That will hit him where he lives if anything will, the boy
thinks, and he goes over it again. "Father I have sinned
against heaven and against you. I am no longer worthy to be
called your son" (Luke 15:18–19), trying to get the inflection
right and the gestures right; and just about the time he
thinks he has it down, the old man spots him coming
around the corner below the tennis court and starts sprinting
down the drive like a maniac. Before the boy has time to get
so much as the first word out, the old man throws his arms
around him and all but knocks him off his feet with the
tears and whiskers and incredulous laughter of his welcome.

The boy is back, that's all that matters. Who cares why
he's back? And the old man doesn't do what any other
father under heaven would have been inclined to do. He
doesn't say he hopes he has learned his lesson or I told you
so. He doesn't say he hopes he is finally ready to settle
down for a while and will find some way to make it up to

his mother. He just says, "Bring him something to eat, for God's sake. Bring him some warm clothes to put on," and when the boy finally manages to slip his prepared remarks in edgewise, the old man doesn't even hear them he's in such a state. All he can say is the boy was dead and is alive again. The boy was lost and is found again, and then at the end of the scene what Jesus as teller of the parable says is "They began to make merry" (Luke 15:23). *Merry*, of all things. They turn on the stereo. They break out the best Scotch. They roll back the living room carpet and ring up the neighbors.

Is it possible, I wonder, to say that it is only when you hear the Gospel as a wild and marvelous joke that you really hear it at all? Heard as anything else, the Gospel is the church's thing, the preacher's thing, the lecturer's thing. Heard as a joke—high and unbidden and ringing with laughter—it can only be God's thing.

And if it is a joke about the preposterousness of God, it is also a joke about the preposterousness of man as the sequel to the parable exemplifies. The word *sin* is somehow too grand a word to apply to the reaction of the prodigal's elder brother when the sound of the hoedown reaches him out in the pasture among the cow flops, and yet in another way it is just the right word because nowhere is the deadliness of all seven of the deadly sins deadlier or more ludicrous than it is in him. Envy and pride and anger and covetousness, they are all there. Even sloth is there as he sits on his patrimony and lets it gain interest for him without lifting a hand, even lust as he slavers over the harlots whom he points out the prodigal has squandered his cash on. The elder brother is Pecksniff. He is Tartuffe. He is what Mark Twain called a good man in the worst sense of the word. He is a caricature of all that is joyless and petty and self-serving about all of us. The joke of it is that of course his father loves him even so, and has always loved him and will always love him, only the elder brother never noticed it because it was never love he was bucking for but only his due. The fatted calf, the best Scotch, the hoedown could all have been his, too, any time he asked for them except that he never thought to ask for them because he was too busy trying cheerlessly and religiously to earn them. "The blind receive their sight, the lame walk, the deaf hear, the dead are raised up" even as the prodigal himself was raised up, Jesus says, "and blessed is he who takes no offense at me" (Matt. 11:5–6). Blessed is he who is not offended that no man receives what he deserves but vastly more. Blessed is he who gets that joke, who sees that miracle.

The ones who don't see it, Jesus says, are the elder brothers, of course, the ones who are blind to comedy because they are too trapped by their own dead seriousness, and again the image he uses, the parable in miniature, has the same kind of sad fun about it, the sad fun of Jewish humor generally—ghetto humor. The religious ones are blind guides, he says, and the ones they are guiding are blind too. They come inching their way down the street together—the guides with their white canes and the ones they are guiding with their cataract lenses thick as the bottoms of Coke bottles. They take the ponderous wooden steps of cigar-store Indians, blind to the fact that there isn't a cloud in the sky and the sun is shining. They are blind to the beauty and wildness of the day and of the world around them. "Is life not more than what you think it is?" Jesus says. "Consider the lilies of the field, how they don't spin or toil or keep accounts and yet Solomon in all the plumage of his honorary doctorates couldn't hold a candle to them" (Matt. 6:28–29). They are blind to each other and to their own deepest needs as human beings, and when the open manhole appears in the pavement before them they are blind to it too and go tumbling headlong with a splash that Abbot and Costello would have been proud of.

People are prepared for everything except for the fact that beyond the darkness of their blindness there is a great light. They are prepared to go on breaking their backs plowing the same old field until the cows come home without seeing, until they stub their toes on it, that there is a treasure buried in that field rich enough to buy Texas. They are prepared for a God who strikes hard bargains but not for a God who gives as much for an hour's work as for a day's. They are prepared for a mustard-seed kingdom of God no bigger than the eye of a newt but not for the great banyan it becomes with birds in its branches singing Mozart. They are prepared for the potluck supper at First Presbyterian but not for the marriage supper of the lamb, and when the bridegroom finally arrives at midnight with vineleaves in his hair, they turn up with their lamps to light him on his way all right only they have forgotten the oil to light them with and stand there with their big, bare, virginal feet glimmering faintly in the dark.

And finally the Gospel itself as comedy—the coming together of Mutt and Jeff, the Captain and the Kids, the Wizard of Oz and the Scarecrow: the coming together of God in his unending greatness and glory and man in his unending littleness, prepared for the worst but rarely for the best, prepared for the possible but rarely for the impossible. The good news breaks into a world where the news has been so bad for so long that when it is good nobody hears it much except for a few. And who are the few that hear it? They are the ones who labor and are heavy-laden like everybody else but who, unlike everybody else, know that they labor and are heavy-laden. They are the last people

you might expect to hear it, themselves the bad jokes and
stooges and scarecrows of the world, the tax collectors and
whores and misfits. They are the poor people, the broken
people, the ones who in terms of the world's wisdom are
children and madmen and fools. They have cut themselves
shaving. Rich or poor, successes or failures as the world
counts it, they are the ones who are willing to believe in
miracles because they know it will take a miracle to fill the
empty place inside them where grace and peace belong with
grace and peace. Old Sarah with her China teeth knows it
will take a miracle to fill the empty place inside her where
she waits for a baby that will never come, so when the
angel appears and tells her a baby is coming she laughs and
Abraham laughs with her because, having used up all their
tears, they have nothing but laughter left. Because although
what the angel says may be too good to be true, who
knows? Maybe the truth of it is that it's too good not to be
true.

Switching on the lectern light and clearing his throat,
the preacher speaks both the word of tragedy and the word
of comedy because they are both of them of the truth and
because Jesus speaks them both, blessed be he. The preacher
tells the truth by speaking of the visible absence of God
because if he doesn't see and own up to the absence of God
in the world, then he is the only one there who doesn't see
it, and who then is going to take him seriously when he
tries to make real what he claims also to see as the invisible
presence of God in the world? Sin and grace, absence and
presence, tragedy and comedy, they divide the world
between them and where they meet head on, the Gospel
happens. Let the preacher preach the Gospel of their
preposterous meeting as the high, unbidden, hilarious thing
it is.

I have spoken of tragedy as inevitable and comedy as

unforeseeable and seen from the inside of each, that seems to me to be so. Charlie Chaplin doesn't see the banana peel on the sidewalk before him whereas Job knows from the start that in his contention with God he is doomed to defeat. But seen from the outside, seen as God sees it and as occasionally by the grace of God man also sees it, I suspect that it is really the other way around. From the divine perspective, I suspect that it is the tragic that is seen as not inevitable whereas it is the comic that is bound to happen. The comedy of God's saving the most unlikely people when they least expect it, the joke in which God laughs with man and man with God—I believe that this is what is inevitable and that this is what King Lear glimpses when at the end of his tragic life, when the world has done its worst, he says to the daughter he loves, " . . . Come, let's away to prison; / We two alone . . . / so we'll live, / And pray, and sing, and tell old tales, and laugh . . ." (5.3.8–12).

IV... The Gospel as Fairy Tale

ONCE upon a time there was a great wizard who lived in a far country. Once upon a time, in a deep forest, there was a poor woodchopper and his wife. Once upon a time a deep sleep fell upon all the inhabitants of the palace, and spiders spun their webs like silver curtains across all the windows and in the throne room, where once the king held court, birds flew in to build their nests and red squirrels came in to store their acorns because in all the place there was no man left awake to hinder them. *Once upon a time,* which is to say at a time beyond time, or at a different kind of time altogether from the kind the clock measures, or at a time that is no time at all because it is without beginning and without end. *There was* a wizard, a woodchopper, a king, which is to say that if you are to believe that *there was,* you have to give up other beliefs you believe in including the

belief that *there was not* because there could not be such
creatures as these. *A far country, a deep forest, a palace,* which is
to say that if you care to enter these places for yourself, you
must be willing to enter them in some measure as a child
because it takes a child to believe in the possibility at least
that such places exist instead of dismissing them
out-of-hand as impossible.

Once upon a time there was a child named Lucy, who
was playing hide-and-seek with some other children in an
old house. It was her turn to be It, and finding herself in a
room where there was no furniture except for a big
old-fashioned wardrobe, and hearing the sound of the others
clattering down the corridor in search of her, she stepped
into the wardrobe to hide. There were clothes hanging in it
and mothballs on the floor, and as she moved farther in
toward the back of it, she could feel the clothes brushing
against her face and arms and could hear the sound of the
mothballs under her feet. C. S. Lewis writes:

> It was almost quite dark in there, and she kept her arms
> stretched out in front of her so as not to bump her face
> into the back of the wardrobe. She took a step farther
> in—then two or three steps—always expecting to feel
> woodwork against the tip of her fingers. But she could
> not feel it. "This must be a simply enormous
> wardrobe," thought Lucy, going still farther in and
> pushing the soft folds of the coats aside to make room
> for her. Then she noticed that there was something
> crunching under her feet. "I wonder is that more
> mothballs?" she thought, stooping down to feel it with
> her hands. But instead of feeling the hard, smooth
> wood of the floor of the wardrobe, she felt something

soft and powdery and extremely cold. "This is very queer," she said, and went on a step or two farther. Next moment she found that what was rubbing against her face and hands was no longer soft fur but something hard and rough and even prickly. "Why, it's just like the branches of trees!" exclaimed Lucy. And then she saw that there was a light in front of her; not a few inches away where the back of the wardrobe ought to have been, but a long way off. Something cold and soft was falling on her. A moment later she found she was standing in the middle of a wood at night-time with snow under her feet and snowflakes falling through the air.[9]

Or in George MacDonald's tale *Fantastes* the hero, Anodos, is awakened by the sound of water and opens his eyes to find that a clear brook is running through his bedroom. The carpet has turned to grass that bends and sways in the light breeze and the furniture is all entwined with ivy. The curtains of his bed have become the branches of a great tree whose leaves are dappling him with shadow. The tree is at the edge of a dense forest, and there are faint traces of a footpath much overgrown with grass and moss leading into it. Or Alice, drowsing by the fire with her cat, notices that the looking glass over the mantle has a curious look to it so she climbs up on the mantle to see, and sure enough the glass starts to melt away like a bright, silvery mist, and she steps through it. Or a farmhouse is caught up in a cyclone and whirled up higher and higher into the stormy sky until finally it comes to rest again and the child inside opens the door onto the Land of Oz.

As far as I know, there has never been an age that has not produced fairy tales. It doesn't seem to matter what is going on at the time. It can be a time of war or peace, of feast or famine. It can be Calvin's Geneva or Calvin Coolidge's U.S.A. No matter what's up politically, economically, religiously, artistically, people always seem to go on telling these stories, many of them stories that have been around for so long that it is as impossible to be sure when they first started as it is to be sure when if ever they will finally end. Different as they are from each other, they seem to have certain features in common, and since more than any other kind of literary form I can think of they come not necessarily from literary people but just from people generally, the way dreams come, there seems reason to believe that if nothing else, they have something to tell us about the kind of things we keep on dreaming century after century, in good times and bad. We keep on telling them to our children and remembering them so well out of our own childhood, that we don't have to look them up and read them out of books most of the time but can simply dredge them up out of ourselves because to one degree or another they have become part of who we are. For my own tastes, it is both more difficult and less interesting to try to explain what fairy tales mean—as a psychologist or a mythologist might—than it is simply to look at them for what they contain. Like the world of dreams or the world of memory, the world of the fairy tale is one of the worlds where most of us have at one time or another lived whether we read fairy tales as children or read them still or not because Cinderella and the Sleeping Beauty are part of the air we breathe, and my inclination is to approach their world not as some kind of archaeologist, trying to excavate and analyze, but simply as a tourist guide, trying only to describe some of the principal sights to be seen.

To start with, the stories that do not just tell us about

the world of the fairy tale in and of itself but tell us
something about where it is located and how to reach it,
most, if not all of them, seem to agree that it is not as far
away as we might think and under the right circumstances
not really all that hard to get to. The house where the
children are playing hide-and-seek is an ordinary house just
as the tent where Abraham and Sarah laughed until the
tears ran down their cheeks was an ordinary tent. The
young man Anodos woke up in his bedroom just as he'd
awakened there hundreds of times before, and there was
nothing particularly unusual about the time and place where
Alice curled up beside the fire with her cat, Dinah, any more
than there was anything particularly unusual about Alice
herself living in Victorian London or about Dorothy Gale
living in turn-of-the-century Kansas or about the cyclone
that came twisting across the prairie as cyclones had often
come before and come still. The fairy-tale world that they
all stepped into was very different from the world they
normally lived in and very different, too, from the ordinary
world of who they were inside themselves, their inner
worlds, but the point seems to be that they did not have to
go a great distance to enter it any more than you have to go
a great distance to enter the world of dreams—you just have
to go to sleep—or the world of memory—you just have to
cast your mind's eye backward and let it float up out of the
past.

It might be more accurate to say that the world of the
fairy tale found them, and found them in the midst of their
everyday lives in the everyday world. It is as if the world of
the fairy tale impinges on the ordinary world the way the
dimension of depth impinges on the two-dimensional
surface of a plane, so that there is no point on the plane—a
Victorian sitting room or a Kansas farm—that can't become

an entrance to it. You enter the extraordinary by way of the ordinary. Something you have seen a thousand times you suddenly see as if for the first time like the looking glass over the mantle or the curtains of the bed. Furthermore, even the fairy tales that do not describe the actual passing from one world to the other as such tell about people who though they come in more exotic guise than most of us— poor woodchoppers and fair maidens—are people more or less like ourselves who suddenly, usually without warning, find themselves on the dim frontier. A bankrupt merchant picks a rose for his beautiful daughter and suddenly hears the terrible voice of a beast at his side. A brother and a sister lost in the wood come unexpectedly on a house made of gingerbread. Cinderella, who lives in a loneliness and despair all too familiar, is visited by an old woman who changes a pumpkin into a golden coach. In each case, a strange world opens up when it chooses to open up, and when they enter it things happen that in the inner world of who they are and the outer world of where they ordinarily live their lives couldn't possibly happen.

And what is it like, this world itself, once they have entered it? Maybe the first thing to say is that it is a world full of darkness and danger and ambiguity. Almost the first thing that Lucy's brother Edmund sees when he too steps through the wardrobe into Narnia is a sleigh being pulled through the deep snow by reindeer and seated in the sleigh, wrapped in furs, a queen with a face white as death who holds the whole land under her icy sway. There are fierce dragons that guard the treasure and wicked fairies who show up at royal christenings. To take the wrong turning of the path is to risk being lost in the forest forever, and an awful price has to be paid for choosing the wrong casket or the wrong door. It is a world of dark and dangerous quest

where the suitors compete for the hand of the king's
daughter with death to the losers, or the young prince
searches for the princess who has slept for a hundred years,
or the scarecrow, the tinman, and the lion travel many a
mile in search of the wizard who will make them whole,
and all of them encounter on their way great perils that are
all the more perilous because they are seldom seen for what
they are. That is another mark of the fairy-tale world. The
beautiful queen is really a witch in disguise, and to open the
lid of the golden casket is to be doomed. Not only does evil
come disguised in the world of the fairy tale but often good
does too. Who could guess that the little gray man asking
for bread is a great magician who holds in his hands the
power of life and death? One thinks again of *King Lear,*
which is itself a kind of fairy tale with the two wicked
sisters and the one good one, and like the three rings or the
three caskets, the three speeches each must make about how
they love the old king, their father. In the world of *King Lear*
it is the wicked ones like Goneril and Regan who go about
in gorgeous robes, and the good ones, the compassionate and
innocent ones, who wander disguised in a fool's motley or
the rags of beggars and madmen.

Beasts talk and flowers come alive and lobsters quadrille
in the world of the fairy tale, and nothing is apt to be what
it seems. And if this is true of the creatures that the hero
meets on his quest, it is true also of the hero himself who at
any moment may be changed into a beast or a stone or a
king or have his heart turned to ice. Maybe above all they
are tales about transformation where all creatures are
revealed in the end as what they truly are—the ugly
duckling becomes a great white swan, the frog is revealed to
be a prince, and the beautiful but wicked queen is
unmasked at last in all her ugliness. They are tales of

transformation where the ones who live happily ever after, as by no means everybody does in fairy tales, are transformed into what they have it in them at their best to be.

The Beast falls sick for love of Beauty and lies dying in his garden when she abandons him until she returns out of compassion and says that for all his ugliness she loves him and will marry him, and no sooner has she kissed him on his glistening snout than he himself becomes beautiful with royal blood in his veins. In "The Happy Hypocrite" Max Beerbohm tells about a regency rake named Lord George Hell, debauched and profligate, who falls in love with a saintly girl, and, in order to win her love, covers his bloated features with the mask of a saint. The girl is deceived and becomes his bride, and they live together happily until a wicked lady from Lord George Hell's wicked past turns up to expose him for the scoundrel she knows him to be and challenges him to take off his mask. So sadly, having no choice, he takes it off, and lo and behold beneath the saint's mask is the face of the saint he has become by wearing it in love. The scarecrow gets his brain from the great and terrible Oz, the lion his courage, the tinman his heart. Even in Hans Christian Andersen's "The Steadfast Tin Soldier," one of the darkest of his tales, the theme of the transformed hero is repeated. With only one leg to stand on and battered by his misadventures, the tin soldier remains so steadfast in his love for the paper doll that even after the little boy hurls him in the stove and the flames have melted him, what the servant girl finds in the ashes is a piece of tin in the shape of a heart. For better or worse, in the world of the fairy tale transformations are completed, and one thinks of the angel in the book of Revelation who gives to each a white stone with a new name written on it which is the true and hidden name that he was named with even from the foundations of the world.

To moralize or allegorize these tales or to explain them as having to do with sexual awakening or the successful resolution of Oedipal conflicts is not so much to go too far with them as it is not to go far enough because beneath whatever with varying degrees of success they can be shown to mean, and beneath the specific events and adventures they describe, what gives them their real power and meaning is the world they evoke. It is a world of magic and mystery, of deep darkness and flickering starlight. It is a world where terrible things happen and wonderful things too. It is a world where goodness is pitted against evil, love against hate, order againt chaos, in a great struggle where often it is hard to be sure who belongs to which side because appearances are endlessly deceptive. Yet for all its confusion and wildness, it is a world where the battle goes ultimately to the good, who live happily ever after, and where in the long run everybody, good and evil alike, becomes known by his true name.

It is perhaps this aspect of the fairy tale that gives it its greatest power over us, this sense we have that in that world, as distinct from ours, the marvelous and impossible thing truly happens. No one speaks of this quality more eloquently than one of the great modern masters of the fairy tale J.R.R. Tolkien. He writes that the fairy tale

> . . . does not deny the existence of . . . sorrow and failure: the possibility of these is necessary to the joy of the deliverance; it denies (in the face of much evidence, if you will) universal final defeat . . ., giving a fleeting glimpse of Joy, Joy beyond the walls of the world, poignant as grief.

It is the mark of the good fairy-story, of the higher or more complete kind, that however wild its events, however fantastic or terrible the adventures, it can give to child or man that hears it, when the "turn" comes, a catch of the breath, a beat and lifting of the heart, near to (or indeed accompanied by) tears, as keen as that given by any form of literary art.[10]

Good and evil meet and do battle in the fairy-tale world much as they meet and do battle in our world, but in fairy tales the good live happily ever after. That is the major difference. So great is the power of magic that even the less-than-good live happily ever after. It is the beast who becomes beautiful, the cowardly lion who becomes brave, the wicked sisters with their big feet and fancy ways who repent in the end and are forgiven. It is really two impossible things that happen because happiness is not only inevitable, it is also endless. Joy happens, to use Tolkien's word, and the fairy tale where it happens is not a world where everything is sweetness and light. It is not Disney Land where everything is kept spotless and all the garbage is trundled away through underground passages beneath the sunny streets. On the contrary, the world where this Joy happens is as full of darkness as our own world, and that is why when it happens it is as poignant as grief and can bring tears to our eyes. It can bring tears to our eyes because it might so easily not have happened, and because there are the wicked ones to whom it does not happen, and just because there are some to whom it does not happen, it happens in a world where those who live happily ever after must do so in a world where though happiness is both inevitable and endless, darkness persists because happiness is not universal. Dark spells can still be cast and bad witches prosper. In Tolkien's *The Lord of the Rings,* it is true that in the destruction of the demonic ring a great evil is destroyed, but the universal triumph of good is still only a hobbit's dream, and the golden age of elves and dwarfs is fated to be followed by the tragic age of men. Yet the tears that come to our eyes at the joy of the fairy tale are nevertheless essentially joyous tears because what we have caught a glimpse of, however fleeting, is Joy itself, the triumph if not of goodness, at least of hope. And I do not think it is entirely fanciful to say that it is not only in fairy tales that we have glimpsed it.

You wake up on a winter morning and pull up the shade, and what lay there the evening before is no longer there—the sodden gray yard, the dog droppings, the tire tracks in the frozen mud, the broken lawn chair you forgot to take in last fall. All this has disappeared overnight, and what you look out on is not the snow of Narnia but the snow of home, which is no less shimmering and white as it falls. The earth is covered with it, and it is falling still in silence so deep that you can hear its silence. It is snow to be shoveled, to make driving even worse than usual, snow to be joked about and cursed at, but unless the child in you is entirely dead, it is snow, too, that can make the heart beat faster when it catches you by surprise that way, before your defenses are up. It is snow that can awaken memories of things more wonderful than anything you ever knew or dreamed.

If you still have something more than just eyes to see with, the world can give you these glimpses as well as fairy tales can—the smell of rain, the dazzle of sun on white clapboard with the shadows of ferns and wash on the line, the wildness of a winter storm when in the house the flame of a candle doesn't even flicker. The world can give us such

glimpses, and dreams can too sometimes—the dreams you
wake up from without being quite able to remember them
yet with the knowledge that you are somehow the better for
having dreamed them, dreams that erase old hurts and
failures and start a kind of healing, dreams where the old
man who had his last birthday all those summers ago is
alive and well still. He is wearing a paper hat and nods at
you as if you had met only yesterday, and his death turns
out to have had no more substance to it than the smoke
from his fifty-cent cigar.

The joy beyond the walls of the world more poignant
than grief. Even in church you catch glimpses of it
sometimes though church is apt to be the last place because
you are looking too hard for it there. It is not apt to be so
much in the sermon that you find it or the prayers or the
liturgy but often in something quite incidental like the
evening the choral society does the Mozart *Requiem,* and
there is your friend Dr. X, who you know thinks the whole
business of religion is for the birds, singing the Kyrie like a
bird himself—*Lord, have mercy, have mercy*—as he stands there
among the baritones in his wilted shirt and skimpy tux; and
his workaday basset-hound face is so alive with if not the
God he wouldn't be caught dead believing in then at least
with his twin brother that for a moment nothing in the
whole world matters less than what he believes or doesn't
believe—*Kyrie eleison, Christe eleison*—and as at snow, dreams,
certain memories, at fairy tales, the heart leaps, the eyes
fill.

Here and there and not just in books we catch glimpses
of a world of once upon a time and they lived happily ever
after, of a world where there is a wizard to give courage and
a heart, an angel with a white stone that has written on it
our true and secret name, and it is so easy to dismiss it all

that it is hardly worth bothering to do. It is sentimentality.
It is wishful thinking. It is escapism. It is dodging the issue
and whistling in the dark and childish. And amen we have
to say to the whole cheerless litany because there is not one
of us who does not know it by heart and because there is
not one of us either who does not know that all these things
are part of the truth of it. But if the world of the fairy tale
and our glimpses of it here and there are only a dream, they
are one of the most haunting and powerful dreams that the
world has ever dreamed and no world more than our
twentieth-century one.

Why do we spend vast sums of money to go to the
moon and Mars? You hear all kinds of solemn talk about
learning this and that from it, about beating the Russians to
the draw, about establishing colonies for one purpose or
another; but anybody who knows anything, any child, at
least the child in any of us, knows that we go shooting off
into space because just possibly, impossibly, the Wizard of
Oz is there. The great listening devices that we train on the
skies to catch some whisper of speech from the stars we
even name for a fairy princess and call it Project Ozma. We
hardly need Jung to tell us that whether or not they actually
exist, our fascination with flying saucers reflects our deep
hunger for the wholeness that lies east of the sun and west
of the moon, those great mandalas that float through the sky
with healing in their wings; and we hardly need Erich von
Daniken or Stanley Kubrick to tell us that maybe they have
already landed and built the pyramids for us and taught us
wisdom and as much humanity as we have yet learned and
even intermarried with us maybe so that we have their
blood in our veins, and when we look up at the distant stars
we know, as we have always dimly guessed, that more even
than the earth they are home.

We do our twenty minutes of meditation a day in the hope that, properly stilled, our minds will stop just reflecting back to us the confusion and multiplicity of our world but will turn to a silvery mist like Alice's looking glass that we can step through into a world where the beauty that sleeps in us will come awake at last. We send scientific expeditions to Loch Ness because if the dark and monstrous side of fairy tales can be proved to exist, who can be sure that the blessed side doesn't exist, too? I suspect that the whole obsession of our time with the monstrous in general—with the occult and the demonic, with exorcism and black magic and the great white shark—is at its heart only the shadow side of our longing for the beautific, and we are like the knight in Ingmar Bergman's film *The Seventh Seal,* who tells the young witch about to be burned at the stake that he wants to meet the devil her master, and when she asks him why, he says, "I want to ask him about God. He, if anyone, must know."

I remember a British film that came out of World War II that has a scene in it showing a couple of air-raid wardens sitting out on the roof of a building in London during the blitz. It is night and enemy planes are overhead. Bombs are falling and much of the city is on flames. There are the sounds of antiaircraft guns and sirens. Then, during a lull, one of the men turns to the other and recites a speech of Caliban's out of *The Tempest:*

> Be not afear'd: this isle is full of noises,
> Sounds and sweet airs, that give delight and hurt not:
> Sometimes a thousand twangling instruments
> Will hum about mine ears, and sometimes voices,
> That, if I then had wak'd after long sleep,
> Will make me sleep again: and then, in dreaming,
> The clouds methought would open and show riches

> Ready to drop upon me; that, when I wak'd,
> I cried to dream again.
>
> [3.2.144–55]

Caliban, the earthbound, the spawn of darkness, cries to
dream again about joy beyond the walls of the world, and
in the midst of Armageddon the British air-raid warden
dreams it, and childish, escapist, impossible as it may be, we
dream it, too. And Shakespeare himself, of course, dreamed
it. *King Lear* is a dark fairy tale because though they all
receive their true names in the end, they do not all live
happily ever after, the good ones. Lear, Gloucester, Kent, the
Fool, all die of broken hearts in the end and Cordelia is
hanged by grotesque accident because word does not reach
her jailers in time that her army has been victorious.

But at the close of his career, after the period of the
great tragedies, Shakespeare turned to something much
closer to true fairy tales. He wrote *Cymbeline,* where
innocence is vindicated and old enemies reconciled, and *The
Winter's Tale,* where the dead queen turns out not to be dead
at all, the lost child, Perdita, restored to those who love her.
And he wrote *The Tempest* itself, where the same great storm
of the world that drowned the Franciscan nuns aboard the
Deutschland and lashed old Lear to madness and stung Job in
his despair is stilled by Prospero's magic; and justice is done,
and lovers reunited, and the kingdom restored to its rightful
king so that in a way it is the beautiful dream of Caliban
that turns out to be real and the storm of the world with all
its cloud-capped towers and gorgeous palaces and solemn
temples that turns out to be the insubstantial pageant that
fades into thin air and leaves not a rack behind.

Like the last self-portraits of Rembrandt, where the
ravaged old face of the painter smiles out of the shadows, it

is as if at the end of his career Shakespeare comes out on
the far side of the tragic vision of *Lear* and *Macbeth* and
speaks into the night a golden word too absurd perhaps to
be anything but true, the laughter of things beyond the
tears of things.

The biographer of Henry Ward Beecher tells us that on
his travels he often carried with him a pocketful of precious
stones. People would give them to him, or jewelers, knowing
his taste, would lend them to him, and he would take them
out and look at them and hand them around at the places
he went. Garnets and cat's eyes and pearls, sometimes even
sapphires and emeralds, he called them his "unfading
flowers" and "loved to watch the colors come and go in
their cryptic depths as a child might." Looking at one of
them once, he said that he felt "as if there were a soul back
of it looking through the rays of light flashing over it and in
every way it seemed a thing of life."[11]

I wonder if there is any real doubt what it was that he
saw in them or what the world was whose light gleamed up
at him out of their glittering depths. "Thou hast been in
Eden, the garden of God," the Lord says to Ezekiel. "Every
precious stone was thy covering, the sardius, topaz, and the
diamond, the beryl, the onyx and the jasper, the sapphire,
the emerald, the carbuncle and the gold . . . thou wast upon
the holy mountain of God; thou hast walked up and down
in the midst of the stones of fire" (Ezek. 28:13–14). In
cathedrals and temples, on high altars where the host is
enshrined, there are always jewels like the ones the old
preacher carried around in his pocket or if not jewels, then
stained glass turned to jewels by the sun's shining through
it or the fire of candles as jewels that waver and live. They
are there because in their depth and brilliance they speak of

joy and beauty and holiness beyond the walls of the world. They speak to us of the world of the Gospel as itself the world of the fairy tale.[12]

Like the fairy-tale world, the world of the Gospel is a world of darkness, and many of the great scenes take place at night. The child is born at night. He had his first meal in the dark at his mother's breast, and he had his last meal in the dark too, the blinds drawn and everybody straining to catch the first sound of heavy footsteps on the stair, the first glint of steel in the shadowy doorway. In the garden he could hardly see the face that leaned forward to kiss him, and from the sixth hour to the ninth hour the sun went out like a match so he died in the same darkness that he was born in and rose in it, too, or almost dark, the sun just barely up as it was just barely up again when only a few feet offshore, as they were hauling their empty nets in over the gunnels, they saw him once more standing there barefoot in the sand near the flickering garnets of a charcoal fire.

In the world of the fairy tale, the wicked sisters are dressed as if for a Palm Beach wedding, and in the world of the Gospel it is the killjoys, the phonies, the nitpickers, the holier-than-thous, the loveless and cheerless and irrelevant who more often than not wear the fancy clothes and go riding around in sleek little European jobs marked Pharisee, Corps Diplomatique, Legislature, Clergy. It is the ravening wolves who wear sheep's clothing. And the good ones, the potentially good anyway, the ones who stand a chance of being saved by God because they know they don't stand a chance of being saved by anybody else? They go around looking like the town whore, the village drunk, the crook from the IRS, because that is who they are. When Jesus is asked who is the greatest in the kingdom of Heaven, he reaches into the crowd and pulls out a child with a cheek full of bubble gum and eyes full of whatever a child's eyes are full of and says unless you can become like that, don't bother to ask.

And as for the king of the kingdom himself, whoever would recognize him? He has no form or comeliness. His clothes are what he picked up at a rummage sale. He hasn't shaved for weeks. He smells of mortality. We have romanticized his raggedness so long that we can catch echoes only of the way it must have scandalized his time in the horrified question of the Baptist's disciples, "Are *you* he who is to come?" (Matt. 11:13); in Pilate's "Are you the king of the Jews?" (Matt. 27:11) you with pants that don't fit and a split lip; in the black comedy of the sign they nailed over his head where the joke was written out in three languages so nobody would miss the laugh.

But the whole point of the fairy tale of the Gospel is, of course, that he is the king in spite of everything. The frog turns out to be the prince, the ugly duckling the swan, the little gray man who asks for bread the great magician with the power of life and death in his hands, and though the steadfast tin soldier falls into the flames, his love turns out to be fireproof. There is no less danger and darkness in the Gospel than there is in the Brothers Grimm, but beyond and above all there is the joy of it, this tale of a light breaking into the world that not even the darkness can overcome.

That is the Gospel, this meeting of darkness and light and the final victory of light. That is the fairy tale of the Gospel with, of course, the one crucial difference from all other fairy tales, which is that the claim made for it is that it is true, that it not only happened once upon a time but has kept on happening ever since and is happening still. To preach the Gospel in its original power and mystery is to

claim in whatever way the preacher finds it possible to claim
it that once upon a time is this time, now, and here is the
dark wood that the light gleams at the heart of like a jewel,
and the ones who are to live happily ever after are . . . all
who labor and are heavy laden, the poor naked wretches
wheresoever they be.

Pilate lets the cigarette smoke drift out of his mouth to
screen him a little from the figure before him. Sarah tries to
disguise her first choke of laughter as a cough by covering
her mouth with her apron, and Job sits at the table with his
head in his arms so that he won't have to face the empty
chairs of his children. Poor old Beecher's hand slips, and a
bead of blood swells on his upper lip as he stares at his
reflection in the shaving mirror thinking about the lectures
that he should have gotten together months before and
about little Lib Tilton, his old friend's wife, and about the
small chamois bag in his pocket with an uncut topaz in it,
some pearls, a cat's eye. The preacher holds a knot of black
gown in his fist to keep from tripping as he mounts the
steps to the pulpit, and the high-school math teacher makes
a sharp crease with his thumbnail down the center of his
order of service. Once upon a time is their time, all of them.
They are the ones to live happily everafter. "The joy beyond
the walls of the world more poignant than grief" breaks
through the walls of the world, and like Rumpelstiltskin,
evil is defeated by being named for what it is, and the
world itself receives the true and holy name by which the
master magician calls it to himself.

With his fabulous tale to proclaim, the preacher is
called in his turn to stand up in his pulpit as fabulist
extraordinary, to tell the truth of the Gospel in its highest
and wildest and holiest sense. This is his job, but more often
than not he shrinks from it because the truth he is called to

proclaim, like the fairy tale, seems in all but some kind of wistful, faraway sense too good to be true, and so the preacher as apologist instead of fabulist tries as best he can to pare it down to a size he thinks the world will swallow.

Too good to be true implies a view of truth, of course. It does not have to imply that the truth is bad but only that it is so vast and shapeless and random that it is beyond the power of any adjective to qualify. The truth, reality, is what it is. It is the TV news with the sound turned on and all the other sound turned on with it—the sounds of the house, of the street outside the house, the town, the countryside, the world, the ten thousand times ten thousand worlds of outerspace, and the sound of the great silence and emptiness of space itself. The truth is all the sounds that well up within the preacher as he sits down at his desk to put his sermon together—the sounds of the bills to be paid, the children to educate, the storm windows to put up, the sounds of his own blunders and triumphs, of his lusts and memories and dreams and doubts, any one of which when you come right down to it is apt to seem more real and immediate and clamorous to him than the sound of truth as high and wild and holy. So homiletics become apologetics. The preacher exchanges the fairy-tale truth that is too good to be true for a truth that instead of drowning out all the other truths the world is loud with is in some kind of harmony with them. He secularizes and makes rational. He adapts and makes relevant. He demythologizes and makes credible. And what remains of the fairy tale of the Gospel becomes in his hands a fairy tale not unlike *The Wizard of Oz*.

Thanks to the M-G-M movie, everybody knows the story. The tinman, the lion, the scarecrow, and the child travel many a long mile of yellow-brick road in search of the great wizard who they believe will be able to grant them their hearts' desire: the tinman a heart, the lion courage, the scarecrow a brain, the child a way to get home. After many a perilous adventure, they finally reach the Emerald City, where the wizard lives, and in a devastating audience in which he appears to them variously as a beautiful lady, a terrible beast, a great ball of fire, he tells them that he will do nothing for them until they first destroy the wicked witch and bring him back her broomstick to prove that they have done it. They are almost destroyed themselves in the process, but somehow they manage to bring it off, and when they return with the broomstick to claim their reward, the wizard grants them a second audience. It is a great tragicomic scene. Again the wizard appears to them in all his glory, but instead of granting them their wish, he puts them off and so great is their indignation and disillusion that there is a scuffle in the course of which a screen is knocked over, and there behind the screen is the wizard himself, who turns out to be not a beautiful lady or a terrible beast or a ball of fire, but only a little bald man with a wrinkled face.

Only when they did not see the wizard for what he really was did he appear majestic and beautiful.[13] Only when they did not understand his true nature did they bow down before him as great mystery and power. The Emerald City itself turns out to have looked as if made of emeralds only because they were looking at it through spectacles made of emerald-colored glass. His magic turns out to have been only a series of illusions he worked from behind his screen. In other words, their faith in his power to do anything for them that they could not do for themselves is revealed to be groundless. "You are a very bad man," Dorothy says, and the wizard's answer is, "Oh, no, my dear. I'm really a very good man, but I'm a very bad wizard." So

the great and terrible Oz is only a human being like
Dorothy herself, and the only good he can do for them is a
human good. He cannot give them anything that they do
not already have, and that is the meaning of the gifts he
then distributes among them.

The silk heart stuffed with sawdust that he gives the
tinman, the pins and needles he stuffs inside the scarecrow's
head, the drink out of a saucer that he serves up to the lion,
are only talismans of the heart, the brains, the courage that
they have already acquired by their conscientious pursuit of
them and their defeat of the wicked witch. By bringing out
in them the best that they are, their faith proves to have
been an end in itself and not a means to an unimaginably
greater end. Like a skilled psychotherapist, the wizard helps
them to an inner adjustment that makes them better
equipped to deal with the world as it is, but he is not able
to open up for them or inside of them a world of
transcendence and joy because although he is a very good
man, he is not really a wizard at all. Like people who have
been successfully psychoanalyzed, they are all dressed up
but with no place to go except where they have always
been. The only best for them is the best they can do for
themselves and for each other. As for Dorothy, the wizard
fails her entirely when the balloon he plans to take her back
to Kansas in takes off prematurely without her, but the
story of how the good witch, Glinda, deals with her bears
the same meaning. Glinda tells her that although Dorothy
didn't know it, the silver shoes that she has worn from the
start could have taken her home at any point on her way, so
that, like her three friends, she has had it in her own power
all along to achieve her goal. L. Frank Baum entitles the
chapter of *The Wizard of Oz* in which all this is described
"The Magic Art of the Great Humbug," and they are very
sad and eloquent and suggestive words.

The Wizard of Oz is the fairy tale dehumbugged, and the
good news it bears is the good news that hard and
conscientious effort and a little help from our friends pay off
in the end, and faith is its own reward. The most important
thing to have faith in is ourselves, and that is also the chief
magic. Insofar as they receive their hearts' desire, Dorothy
and her friends, it is essentially a do-it-yourself operation,
and the joy of it is not beyond the walls of the world but
within the walls of the world. The book was published in
the year 1900, and maybe it is not stretching things too far
to say that in a way it foreshadows something of what
became of the fairy tale of the Gospel in the century it
ushered in. The magic and the mystery fade. Like the
Emerald City, the city whose gates are pearl and whose
walls are adorned with jasper and onyx and sapphire turns
out to be too good to be true for all except those who see it
through stained glass; and just as for Dorothy home is
finally not the Land of Oz, where all things are possible, but
Kansas, where never yet has a camel managed to squeeze
through the eye of a needle, so for us home is not that
country that Gideon and Barak, Samson and Jeptha,
glimpsed from afar, but rather just home, just here, where
there are few surprises. As for the one who promises to save
the world, he is in the richest sense a good man to be sure,
but like the little bald man behind the screen, when you
come right down to it not all that much of a wizard. His
goodness, his love, his simple eloquence, touch our hearts
and illumine our darkness across the centuries, but for all of
that, both we and our world remain basically untransformed.
Though he is wizard enough to set us dreaming sometimes
of a world of joy more poignant than grief, we tend to
believe in our hearts that, however holy and precious, it is
only a dream.

For the sake, as he sees it, of the ones he preaches to,

the preacher is apt to preach the Gospel with the high magic
taken out, the deep mystery reduced to a manageable size.
"Ask and it will be given you; seek and you will find;
knock, and it will be opened to you." "Truly, I say to you,
if you have faith as a grain of mustard seed, you will say to
this mountain, Remove hence to yonder place, and it will be
moved and nothing will be impossible to you" (Matt.
17:20). "Come, O blessed of my Father, and inherit the
kingdom prepared for you from the foundation of the
world" (Matt. 35:24). "He who believes in me, though he
die, yet shall he live" (John 11:25). The wild and joyful
promise of the Gospel is reduced to promises more easily
kept. The peace that passeth all understanding is reduced to
peace that anybody can understand. The faith that can move
mountains and raise the dead becomes faith that can help
make life bearable until death ends it. Eternal life becomes a
metaphor for the way the good a man does lives after him.
"Blessed is he who takes no offense at me" (Matt. 11:6),
Jesus says, and the preacher is apt to seek to remove the
offense by removing from the Gospel all that he believes we
find offensive. You cannot blame him because up to a point,
of course, he is right. With part of ourselves we are
offended as he thinks by what is too much for us to believe.
We weren't born yesterday. We are from Missouri.

But we are also from somewhere else. We are from Oz,
from Looking-Glass Land, from Narnia, and from Middle
Earth. If with part of ourselves we are men and women of
the world and share the sad unbeliefs of the world, with a
deeper part still, the part where our best dreams come from,
it is as if we were indeed born yesterday, or almost
yesterday, because we are also all of us children still. No
matter how forgotten and neglected, there is a child in all of
us who is not just willing to believe in the possibility that

maybe fairy tales are true after all but who is to some
degree in touch with that truth. You pull the shade on the
snow falling, white on white, and the child comes to life for
a moment. There is a fragrance in the air, a certain passage
of a song, an old photograph falling out from the pages of a
book, the sound of somebody's voice in the hall that makes
your heart leap and fills your eyes with tears. Who can say
when or how it will be that something easters up out of the
dimness to remind us of a time before we were born and
after we will die? The child in us lives in a world where
nothing is too familiar or unpromising to open up into the
world where a path unwinds before our feet into a deep
wood, and when that happens, neither the world we live in
nor the world that lives in us can ever entirely be home
again any more than it was home for Dorothy in the end
either because in the Oz books that follow *The Wizard,* she
keeps coming back again and again to Oz because Oz, not
Kansas, is where her heart is, and the wizard turns out to be
not a humbug but the greatest of all wizards after all.

So let the preacher remember this and preach to us not
just as men and women of the world but as children, too,
who are often much more simple-hearted than he supposes,
and much hungrier for, and ready to believe in, and already
in contact with, more magic and mystery than most of the
time even we are entirely aware of ourselves. "Unless you
turn and become like children, you will never enter the
kingdom of Heaven" (Matt. 18:3), Jesus says, and he is not
just being sentimental as he says it. Let the preacher stretch
our imagination and strain our credulity and make our jaws
drop because the sad joke of it is that if he does not, then
of all people he is almost the only one left who does not.
Scientists speak of intelligent life among the stars, of how at
the speed of light there is no time, of consciousness as more

than just an epiphenomenon of the physical brain. Doctors speak seriously about life after death, and not just the mystics anymore but the housewife, the stockbroker, the high-school senior speak about an inner world where reality becomes transparent to a reality realer still. The joke of it is that often it is the preacher who as steward of the wildest mystery of them all is the one who hangs back, prudent, cautious, hopelessly mature and wise to the last when no less than Saint Paul tells him to be a fool for Christ's sake, no less than Christ tells him to be a child for his own and the kingdom's sake.

Let the preacher tell the truth. Let him make audible the silence of the news of the world with the sound turned off so that in that silence we can hear the tragic truth of the Gospel, which is that the world where God is absent is a dark and echoing emptiness; and the comic truth of the Gospel, which is that it is into the depths of his absence that God makes himself present in such unlikely ways and to such unlikely people that old Sarah and Abraham and maybe when the time comes even Pilate and Job and Lear and Henry Ward Beecher and you and I laugh till the tears run down our cheeks. And finally let him preach this overwhelming of tragedy by comedy, of darkness by light, of the ordinary by the extraordinary, as the tale that is too good not to be true because to dismiss it as untrue is to dismiss along with it that catch of the breath, that beat and lifting of the heart near to or even accompanied by tears, which I believe is the deepest intuition of truth that we have.

Notes

1. Lyman Abbott, *Henry Ward Beecher* (Hartford: American Publishing Co., 1887), p. 210.
2. Frederick Buechner, *Open Heart* (New York: Atheneum, 1972), pp. 97–101.
3. Herman Melville, *Moby Dick* (New York: Random House, 1930), p. 68.
4. *Ibid.*, p. 282.
5. W. H. Gardner and N. H. MacKenzie, eds., *The Poetry of Gerard Manley Hopkins,* 4th rev. ed. (London: Oxford University Press, 1967), pp. 51–63.
6. Stephen Crane, *War Is Kind* (New York: Stokes, 1899), p. 56.
7. Gardner and MacKenzie, eds., p. 106.
8. *Ibid.*, p. 107.
9. C. S. Lewis, *The Lion, the Witch, and the Wardrobe* (New York: Collier Books, 1975), pp. 5–7.
10. J. R. R. Tolkien, *The Tolkien Reader* (New York: Ballantine, 1966), pp. 68–69.
11. Lyman Abbott, pp. 198–201, and Paxton Hibben, *Henry Ward Beecher* (New York: Readers' Club Edition, 1942), p. 178.

12. For a more extensive discussion of this, see Aldous Huxley, *The Doors of Perception and Heaven and Hell* (London: Penguin Books), pp. 84–89.
13. For this discussion I am indebted to Michael Patrick Hearn, *The Annotated Wizard of Oz* (New York: Potter, 1973). See especially his notes on chapter 15.